This book is to be returned on or before
the last date stamped below.

IN PURSUIT

OF
EXCELLENCE

HOW TO WIN IN SPORT AND LIFE
THROUGH MENTAL TRAINING

THIRD EDITION

TERRY ORLICK, PHD

Rev. 03124 new copy on order.

WEST SUFFOLK HOSPITAL
LIBRARY

T09936

Human Kinetics

Library of Congress Cataloging-in-Publication Data

Orlick, Terry.
  In pursuit of excellence : how to win in sport and life through mental training / Terry Orlick--3rd ed.
    p. cm.
  Includes bibliographical references (p.) and index.
  ISBN 0-7360-3186-3
    1. Sports--Psychological aspects. I. Title.

GV706.4.O73   2000
796'.01--dc21

                                         00-024335

ISBN: 0-7360-3186-3

Copyright © 2000, 1990, 1980 by Terry Orlick

All rights reserved. Except for use in a review, the reproduction or utilization of this work in any form or by any electronic, mechanical, or other means, now known or hereafter invented, including xerography, photocopying, and recording, and in any information storage and retrieval system, is forbidden without the written permission of the publisher.

Managing Editor: Melinda Graham; **Assistant Editor:** John Wentworth; **Consultant:** Kelly Hill; **Copyeditor:** Jacqueline Eaton Blakley; **Proofreader:** Susan C. Hagan; **Indexer:** Craig Brown; **Graphic Designer:** Nancy Rasmus; **Graphic Artist:** Francine Hamerski; **Photo Editor:** Clark Brooks; **Cover Designer:** Jack W. Davis; **Photographer (cover):** Tom Roberts; **Illustrator:** Craig Newsom; **Printer:** United Graphics

Human Kinetics books are available at special discounts for bulk purchase. Special editions or book excerpts can also be created to specification. For details, contact the Special Sales Manager at Human Kinetics.

Printed in the United States of America   10 9 8 7 6 5 4

Human Kinetics
Web site: www.humankinetics.com

United States: Human Kinetics
P.O. Box 5076
Champaign, IL 61825-5076
800-747-4457
e-mail: humank@hkusa.com

Canada: Human Kinetics
475 Devonshire Road, Unit 100
Windsor, ON N8Y 2L5
800-465-7301 (in Canada only)
e-mail: orders@hkcanada.com

Europe: Human Kinetics
Units C2/C3 Wira Business Park
West Park Ring Road
Leeds LS16 6EB, United Kingdom
+44 (0)113 278 1708
e-mail: hk@hkeurope.com

Australia: Human Kinetics
57A Price Avenue
Lower Mitcham, South Australia 5062
08 8277 1555
e-mail: liahka@senet.com.au

New Zealand: Human Kinetics
P.O. Box 105-231, Auckland Central
09-523-3462
e-mail: hkp@ihug.co.nz

PART IV LIVING EXCELLENCE

ACKNOWLEDGMENTS

To the thousands of athletes, coaches, students, and great performers in many different disciplines who have challenged me to give my best and allowed me to continue to learn and grow as they have explored their own potential. To my wonderful wife, Bellsa, for her passion, and to little Jewelia for her daily reminders to embrace pure and simple joys. To Claudette Ladouceur and Melinda Graham for helping me make the final revisions for this book. Thank you all for the ways in which you have enriched my perspectives and my life.

Part I

Visions of Excellence

CHAPTER 1

THE WHEEL OF EXCELLENCE

Excellence in performance and in life begins with a vision of where you want to go and a commitment to do what it takes to get there. My life's work with thousands of performers has led me to a clear understanding of what is required to make this journey successfully. There are seven critical elements of excellence that guide your pursuit of personal excellence: *commitment, focused connection, confidence, positive images, mental readiness, distraction control,* and *ongoing learning.* These elements, which make up the *wheel of excellence,* provide the mental keys that empower you to excel and free you to become the person and performer you really want to be. The great news is that each of these elements of excellence is within your potential control (see figure 1.1).

MY GOAL IN WRITING THIS BOOK IS TO FREE YOU TO BECOME THE PERSON AND PERFORMER YOU CAN BE—TO EMPOWER YOU TO CONSISTENTLY LIVE AND PERFORM CLOSER TO YOUR POTENTIAL.

We are all performers living the drama of life in different contexts. We are all capable of pursuing our dreams and reaching our goals. We all possess unlimited strength within the power of our minds. By developing the seven elements of excellence, we create the quality and consistency of our own performance and enrich our own lives.

The heart of human excellence often begins to beat when you discover a pursuit that gives you a sense of meaning, joy, or passion. When you find something within a pursuit, or within yourself, that you are truly committed to develop, everything else can grow. The soul of human excellence grows naturally through a confident focus and an absolute connection to each step in the moment-by-moment pursuit. It is this focused connection that frees you to continue to learn, experiment, create, enjoy, and perform to your capacity.

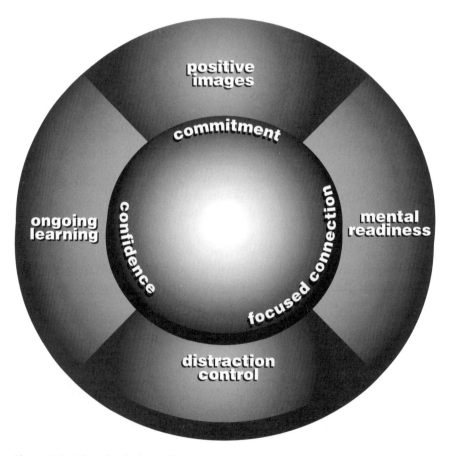

Figure 1.1 The wheel of excellence.

COMMITMENT

The first element of excellence is your *commitment* to

- pursue your dream or make a meaningful contribution;
- be the best you can be;
- do everything required to excel;
- develop the mental, physical, and technical links to excellence;
- set clear personal goals and relentlessly pursue them;
- persist through the obstacles—even when they appear insurmountable; and
- continue to learn, nurture your passion, and find joy in your pursuit.

Commitment is the first essential ingredient guiding the pursuit of excellence. With commitment, you can do almost anything; without it, high-level goals are virtually impossible to attain. There are many different sources of commitment that drive excellence, the most basic of which include:

- Pure enjoyment or passion for the pursuit
- The desire to feel competent, needed, valued, important, successful, or special
- The quest to fulfill your potential, become what you are capable of becoming, or make a meaningful contribution
- Pride in your performance or creation
- The joy or love of ongoing learning

Excellence is inspired by having, or creating, a positive vision of where you want to go—in your sport or performance domain, or in your life outside of your performance. To excel at any challenging pursuit you must have, or develop, a reason for doing it, a passion for your pursuit. High levels of commitment grow naturally out of positive visions and love for, or joy in, what you are doing—but there are also tough parts, and not everything is joyful. Commitment grows from embracing special moments, giving yourself to your mission, and loving the experience of ongoing personal growth. If you like what you are doing (or at least parts of it) and are able to remain committed to it, you will become very competent at it—which is a very worthy and beneficial goal. To become truly great at it, and to continue to perform at high levels over extended periods of time, you usually have to love it. For most performers who excel at the highest levels, the pursuit itself becomes their passion and drives their lives, at least for certain extended periods of time. They are truly passionate about their pursuits. They love the joyful parts of what they are doing and draw positive energy from the pursuit, which helps them to reach their goals and benefit from the journey.

Feelings of self-fulfillment, confidence, and worthy contribution come through the day-to-day process of engaging yourself in your mission, overcoming obstacles, finding simple joys, and embracing personal growth along the way. Excellence results from acting daily in ways that lead you to excel—step by step. This means committing yourself to ongoing high-quality preparation and connecting fully with the step in front of you. The ultimate goal is to connect fully for the duration of your action, interaction, or performance. Excellence requires that you persist through the ups and downs associated with becoming your best and that you find ways of maintaining your best perspective. There will be times when the obstacles seem insurmountable. Every person experiences this, even the greatest performers. If you think the obstacles are too great to overcome, you are right even when you are wrong. At times like this, the challenge is to remember your vision or dream, to continue to find passion in parts of your pursuit, and to fully embrace the process of ongoing learning. Persistence and perspective will get you through the obstacles.

Committing adequate time for mental and physical recovery is a critical part of consistent high-level performance. We all need to find a place where we feel free from the demands of performance or life. You must learn to listen to your body and respect your basic needs for relaxation, rest, personal space, good nutrition, and joyful moments away from your performance domain. What you do with your time and focus away from your performance arena has a tremendous effect on what you are able to do within your performance arena. We all benefit from quiet times for rest and reflection—alone, with nature, and with loved ones. If you fail to find a balance between quality work and quality rest, it will eventually destroy you, your performance, or your love for what you are doing. One of the greatest challenges of ongoing excellence lies in respecting your shifting needs for achievement and relaxation, and ensuring that your current commitment is directed toward doing what will be most beneficial for you and your ultimate goals.

FOCUSED CONNECTION

The second element of excellence centers on being *fully focused or completely connected*

- for the duration of your task, performance, or interaction;
- on the task at hand;
- in the moment;
- in your zone;
- in the performance;
- totally absorbed in what you are doing or experiencing;
- on autopilot; and
- freeing yourself to let good things unfold naturally.

In a very real sense, **focus is everything**—in life and in performance pursuits. A positive and absorbing focus channels your commitment into a series of positive actions, thereby making your personal journey to excellence possible. A fully connected focus releases you from everything irrelevant and connects you totally with your experience or performance. It is a mind-place where nothing else in your world exists apart from being totally connected with what you are engaged in or experiencing at that moment. Focusing is the most important mental skill associated with ongoing learning and consistent high-level performance. Your challenge is to discover and perfect a focus that frees you to perform your best and to live that fully connected focus while you are engaged in the task, activity, or performance. The key to consistent high-quality performance is to consistently focus in ways that free you to perform to your capacity within different contexts. The quality of your focus affects every learning and performance situation you encounter. It determines your rate of learning, quality of learning, quality of performance, and quality of life. By guiding your focus in positive ways, you control the intensity, direction, duration, and consistency of your actions and reactions.

A best-performance focus is both absorbing and natural, free-flowing and intense, simple and magical. It is a focus that you lived often as a very young child. The ultimate goal of all preparation and performance is to enter this fully connected zone on a consistent basis. By training your mind to connect fully, trusting your connection, and freeing yourself to let outside worries go, you can live and perform closer to your capacity in situations that count. The key to accomplishing this lies in absorbing yourself in the present—in the here and now—and gradually increasing the consistency, quality, and duration of your focus. When you step out of the performance arena, a simple shift in focus to something less demanding or more relaxing can free you to return with a clearer, stronger, more positive focus.

Your focus is the leader. Where your focus goes, everything else follows. Let it lead wisely.

CONFIDENCE

The third element of excellence is *confidence, trust,* or *belief* in

- your own potential;
- your capacity to overcome obstacles and achieve your goals;
- your preparation or readiness;
- your focus;
- your choices;
- the meaningfulness of your mission or pursuit; and
- those with whom you work or play.

Confidence is the third essential ingredient guiding the pursuit of excellence. Performance confidence rises or falls based on the quality of your experiences and the extent to which you develop your mental strengths. Confidence comes from committing yourself to do the preparation or quality work, talking to yourself in positive ways about what you have done and what you can do, drawing lessons from your experiences and acting on them, and remaining positive with yourself through the many challenges and struggles along the way. Confidence grows when you discover what focus works best for you and regularly call upon that focus.

Where there is unwavering belief in your capacity to carry out a mission and absolute connection with your performance, doors are opened to higher levels of excellence. When negative experiences or negative thoughts interfere with your confidence, your performance wavers—not because you are any less capable, but because you let those doubts interfere with your best focus and limit your real possibilities. Pure confidence comes from feeling grounded in who you are and what you are doing. In the presence of pure confidence, you trust your focus, and your performance blossoms; in its absence, you rarely touch your full potential. To strengthen your confidence:

- Remember that someone believes in you.
- Think in positive ways about your capacity.
- Act as if you can do it.
- Engage in high-quality technical, physical, and mental preparation.
- Recall your successes from training, simulations, and performances.
- Look for the positive parts of all experiences and performances.
- Continually draw out constructive lessons to improve the quality and consistency of your performances.

We rarely begin pursuits with total confidence in our capacity to achieve our goals or execute tasks with precision. We often do not know what we are really capable of doing. Rookie surgeons in an operating theater and rookie athletes in a competition arena acquire confidence through experiences in practice and performance. We grow by acknowledging our improvements, learning from our own successes and failures, and absorbing the wisdom of others.

The only way to win the confidence game is to strengthen your mental skills. Each element on the wheel of excellence can help you to improve the quality of your preparation, the consistency of your performance, and the level of your confidence. When you strengthen your mental skills, your confidence is strengthened and your commitment is enhanced. As your commitment rises, you often give more of yourself and gain more confidence, both of which improve the level and consistency of your performance. Confidence is like a master key: it opens the door to higher levels of excellence, and higher levels of excellence open the door to greater confidence.

You can perform well without feeling confident—if you are able to enter a fully connected focus within your performance. But you are much more likely to perform to your potential on a consistent basis if your confidence and your focus are working together for you. This gift comes from respecting yourself and freeing your body and mind to perform unhindered. Give yourself this gift. You are fully worthy of it.

POSITIVE IMAGES

The fourth element of excellence is using your *imagination* in *positive* ways to

- create inspiration and positive visions;
- target specific daily goals;
- speed up the learning process;
- prepare yourself to follow your game plan and perform to your capacity;
- act and react in more positive ways;
- improve the flawless execution of performance skills; and
- enhance your confidence.

What are your big dreams? What do you want to accomplish in your sport or performance pursuits? What positive things are you going to do today—in and out of your performance arena? How do you want to perform during your next challenge or performance? Think about it. Run it through your mind. Feel it in your body. Positive thoughts and images help create the mind-set and focus for high-quality performance and guide your actions in positive ways.

The world's best performers have highly developed imagery skills that they use daily to create a positive mind-set for excellence. They draw upon positive memories, recall the feelings of previous best performances, and create positive visions of the future. They use their imagery to mentally prepare themselves for quality practice, performances, and joyful life experiences. To improve future performances, they carefully assess both positive and negative parts of their performances and refine their skills in their minds. They think, see, or imagine themselves as competent, confident, successful, and in control, which sets the stage for higher-quality performance. When learning new skills, procedures, or routines, they run through desired actions many times in their minds, with quality, to speed up the learning process. They also use positive imagery skills to relax and regain control when distracted or struggling through obstacles.

The overall benefit of thinking, planning, and guiding your imagination in positive ways is to set a positive frame of mind for living and performing with quality. It allows you to create the conditions for success without having actually executed that performance in the real world. This mental process serves to enhance your confidence, focus, and performance. It leaves you with good feelings about yourself, your readiness, and your capacity to do the things that you want to do. With practice, you can pre-experience and re-experience many desired actions, feelings, sensations, and skills that are important for the successful execution of your performance. Your imagination can take you where you want to go and where you have not yet been.

MENTAL READINESS

The fifth element of excellence is your *mental readiness* to

- create positive learning opportunities;
- take advantage of performance opportunities;
- develop essential mental, physical, and technical skills necessary to excel in your pursuit;
- plan, prepare, and evaluate effectively;
- follow a path that brings out the best in you; and
- relax yourself and your focus away from the performance zone.

Personal excellence requires that you find a way to get the most out of yourself and your experiences—daily—for practices, performances, and ongoing learning. This begins with a commitment to be mentally ready to make the most of each experience and each opportunity. To be mentally ready, you must consistently enter a positive, focused state for learning, performing, or interacting. To excel at anything, you have to learn essential skills, commit to practice those skills to perfection, perform those skills effectively under demanding conditions, and draw lessons from each of your experiences. Excellence emerges when you are mentally ready to act in positive ways. Great performers have very effective action plans or routines to get themselves mentally ready to accomplish whatever they want to do each day and during each performance.

You can prepare yourself mentally by thinking about your goals and about what you are going to do to achieve those goals. What do you want to accomplish today? You might find it helpful to write your goals down and run them through your mind. This can enhance your commitment to act consistently on your goals and plans. Look for simple and effective ways to get yourself mentally ready to enter a quality-focus zone for achieving your daily goals. Developing an action plan and way of thinking that brings you to an ideal state of readiness is essential for ongoing learning and consistent high-level performance. Positive action plans usually include positive images, confidence-enhancing thoughts, and specific reminders of exactly what you want to do and how you can best focus to do it.

The pursuit of excellence is a process of self-discovery and stretching limits, continually acting on discoveries that lead to your best focus and best performances. As you discover what works and feels best for you, remember to follow this path, even in the face of obstacles. Consistent high-level performers are great at following their own best paths. They are superb self-directed learners. They have learned to carry a positive perspective, to respect what works best for them, and to continue to look for ways to improve. With positive planning and persistent positive action, the mind-set for excellence becomes a natural way of being. It leads you to quality and consistent high-level performance.

Before you spring into action you should develop a plan for achieving your goals.

DISTRACTION CONTROL

The sixth element of excellence is developing your skills for *controlling distractions* in order to

- maintain a positive, effective focus in the face of distractions;
- regain an effective focus when distracted before, during, or after an event or performance;
- quickly re-enter your best focus;
- perform consistently at your desired level;
- stick with your own game plan;
- get adequate rest; and
- stay on your own best path for personal excellence.

Once you have learned to connect fully within your performance or experience, even for moderate periods of time, distraction control becomes the most important mental skill affecting the quality and consistency of your performance. *Distraction control* refers to your skills at maintaining or regaining a positive, connected focus when faced with potential distractions, obstacles, negative input, or setbacks. Distractions may be *external,* arising from the people or circumstances in your environment, or *internal,* arising from your own thinking or expectations. Maintaining a positive perspective before and after a performance and regaining a fully connected focus within a performance are critical parts of performing to your capacity on a consistent basis. Distraction control skills are especially important when performing in demanding circumstances or living through high-stress situations. Learning to initiate positive shifts in focus comes most readily from developing a refocusing plan and acting on that plan. When you experience negative thoughts, lapses in concentration, setbacks, or dips in confidence—before, during, or after a performance—the goal is to quickly regain a positive perspective or a fully connected focus. You can learn to reconnect more quickly and effectively by reflecting on what is likely to work best for you to get you back on track, by planning your best path, and by practicing your refocusing plan whenever the opportunity arises. Great performers activate positive shifts in focus by using simple reminders, images, or focus points that reconnect them with something positive or rapidly refocus their attention on what is within their immediate control. This brings them back to where they want to be—to a more positive mind-set and a total connection within the present performance moment. By strengthening your ability to quickly refocus, you will achieve greater consistency in your performance and experience more enjoyment in your life.

Ongoing Learning

The seventh element of excellence is a commitment to and passion for *ongoing learning*, which includes

- reflecting on what you have done well;
- reflecting on what you can refine or improve;
- drawing out important lessons from each experience or performance;
- assessing how your commitment, mental readiness, and focus affected your performance;
- targeting relevant areas for improvement; and
- acting upon lessons learned on an ongoing basis.

Personal excellence results from living the lessons from your experiences. Great performers attain a high level of excellence because they are committed to ongoing learning. They prepare well, do thorough postperformance evaluations, and act on the lessons they draw from their experiences. They acknowledge their good qualities, look for positive parts of their performances, and target areas for improvement. They gain inspiration, confidence, and joy by looking for personal highlights, and continue to reflect upon what frees them to live fully and perform their best. They also draw inspiration from setbacks and channel that energy toward their own improvement.

You can extract important lessons by evaluating your overall performance, critical parts of your performance, and the role that your mental state played in your performance. For example, you can ask yourself: *Was I prepared well enough? Was I mentally ready? Did I focus through the distractions? Did I free myself to connect fully within my performance? Did I sustain my focused connection for the duration of my event or performance?*

Ongoing learning centers on three important actions:

1. Reflecting on what went well and why it went well

2. Targeting relevant areas for continued improvement

3. Acting on the lessons learned

When you commit yourself to initiate these three actions on a regular basis, you optimize your learning opportunities. These actions guide your preparation and your continued pursuit of excellence.

To move toward your true potential, continue to reflect upon the mind-set and focus that you carry into your most joyful experiences and best performances. Continue to refine your focus until it is consistently where you want it to be. In the beginning it may help to write down the lessons you learn from your best and less than best experiences or performances; in the end, it is best if they are recorded in your *mental* notebook. Embrace these lessons, remember them, and act upon them. Your rate of learning, the level and consistency of your performance, and the quality of your life are directly affected by the extent to which you engage in this ongoing process of thorough, constructive, personal evaluation, followed by positive action.

NURTURING EXCELLENCE

I have had the opportunity to work and interact with many of the world's greatest performers, who have excelled in different disciplines. The most striking revelation about these exceptional performers is the extent of their similarities with respect to their highly developed mental skills and positive performance perspectives. Exceptional Asian athletes, all of whom were Olympic or world champions, had performance perspectives and mental skills that were similar to those of exceptional athletes in Canada, the United States, and Europe. Exceptional surgeons and astronauts in North America had performance perspectives and mental strengths similar to those of exceptional classical musicians in Europe and Scandinavia. Though they live in different environments and excel in different domains, they are of one focused performance culture. They all have highly refined wheels of excellence.

It is also worth noting that all great performers, from NHL hockey players to top classical musicians, speak of the important role that fun, joy, passion, or love for the pursuit has played and continues to play in freeing them to excel. The joy of the pursuit enhances their ongoing commitment to their mission and helps them remain positive through the ups and downs of their journeys.

Those who excel at the highest levels are more like you than you might expect. They get nervous or even fearful before they compete or perform in big events. They experience ups and downs in their confidence and sometimes have doubts about their abilities. What separates these people is that they commit themselves fully to develop one area of their lives and persist with the strengthening of key mental skills required to excel in that area. In other parts of their lives they often view themselves as normal or average. Whether your goals are big or modest, the seven elements that make up the wheel of excellence will take you on an exciting journey toward your true potential in your performance domain and in your life. Each of these mental links to excellence has the capacity to strengthen your resolve and bring you nearer your capacity.

The seven links to excellence are closely connected, and each plays a significant role in nurturing ongoing improvement. Commitment provides the fuel that leads you along the path of excellence—day by day, month by month, year after year. A focused connection creates the quality of your learning and the quality of your performance or experience. Positive visions provide the inspiration or inner strength to continue to pursue your goals and dreams.

When you bring commitment and focus to any valued pursuit, you have a great chance of reaching your goals. Commitment and a focused connection lead to positive actions that build your confidence, and confidence in turn strengthens your commitment and focus. Together they open the door to new realities. When you begin to trust your abilities, your preparation, and your focus, you free yourself to connect totally with your performance, to let it go, to perform in your best, most natural way. When confidence wavers, revisit your successes, look for reasons to believe, and recall your best focus. Continue to nurture commitment, connection, and inner confidence to ensure continuous growth and ongoing contribution.

If you commit to developing and refining the mental links to excellence, you will begin to roll forward in a positive direction. Let your vision of where you want to go give concrete direction to your actions. Let your positive images of simple, daily steps provide a specific path and visible goals, and thereby guide your pursuit of excellence. Work on improving your focus day by day, step by step, moment by moment. An absorbing focus makes excellence possible. Take the time to get yourself mentally ready to enter your practice, work, or performance arena in the right frame of mind. Mental readiness empowers you to be consistent in learning and best performances. Develop a plan for distraction control to stay on your desired path and get you back on track when you stray away. Commit yourself to ongoing learning to ensure that you continue to learn and grow in meaningful ways and that you act on the lessons from your experiences every day.

When we fall short of our potential in sport, performance, school, work, relationships, health, or life, it is usually because our mental wheels are running with underdeveloped or untapped parts. Either the heart of our commitment or the soul of our connection is not strong enough, or one of the other elements of excellence is not yet fully developed. This results in an inconsistent or shaky wheel. We need strong mental wheels to guide ourselves to personal excellence.

To attain the goal of personal excellence is to do everything in your power to fulfill your own goals and dreams, to raise the level and consistency of your performance, to experience a greater sense of enjoyment and personal satisfaction in your pursuits, and to enhance the overall quality of your life. A performance goal does not have to become the only thing in your life in order for you to attain it, but it must be the only thing in your life while you are engaged in the process of doing it or performing.

Everyone begins at a different departure point with respect to personal assets. When you develop and stretch those assets, even for short periods of time, you become more fully alive—you touch the essence of personal excellence. By acting on each of the seven elements of excellence, you greatly increase your chances of journeying in positive directions and reaching your own potential.

MAKING THE WHEEL WORK FOR YOU

The wheel of excellence can serve as a personal guide for improving anything that is important in your life. Decide what is most important for you at this time. Then look over the wheel keeping that goal in mind. Assess where you think your mental skills are strongest and where they need strengthening. Target a specific area for improvement that seems most relevant for you at this time. Develop a plan for your own improvement and work on implementing it. Then revisit the wheel to reflect on your progress and to target another area for improvement. The following questions may help you in clarifying your direction.

Commitment

- Are your goals clear, challenging, and targeted at being or contributing your best?
- Are you doing something every day that takes you a step closer to your goals?
- Are you working at improving every day and in every performance?
- Is your commitment to quality in training, learning, practice, preparation, and performing strong enough to help you reach your goals?
- Are you keeping an element of joyfulness in your pursuit and in your life?
- Is your commitment to respect your personal needs for rest and recovery strong enough to sustain you through this challenging journey?

Focused Connection

- Do you know what kind of focus helps you perform best?
- Do you know what kind of focus helps you learn best?
- Do you have a plan to consistently get into this fully connected state?
- Are you working at improving the quality and consistency of your focus? How?
- Are you focusing on doing the little things that work best for you?
- Do you sustain your best focus or best connection for the duration of each class, practice, work session, interaction, or performance? Can you do better? How?

Confidence

- Do you believe you can reach your dreams or attain your goals?
- Are you putting yourself in situations that give you the greatest chance of believing in yourself and achieving your goals?
- Are you looking for the good things in your performance and in your life? Every day?
- Are you seeing your own progress and appreciating it?
- Are you thinking and acting in ways that make you feel positive and confident?

- Are you trusting yourself, your preparation, and your focus? Can you do better?
- Are you allowing your performance to unfold freely?

Positive Images

- Do you have a big vision of where you would like to go with your performance, your profession, or your life? Is that vision clear in your mind?
- Do you visit that big vision regularly?
- Can you imagine yourself performing exactly the way you would like to perform, doing the things you want to do ,or being the way you would prefer to be?
- Do you imagine yourself achieving your goals? Often?
- Do you imagine yourself doing the little things, taking the daily little steps that will bring you to your goals? Every day?
- Are you waking up your positive images by acting on those images in positive ways every day?

Mental Readiness

- Do you carry a positive mind-set into your work sessions, interactions, practices, and performances? Always?
- Do you look for opportunities in everything?
- Are you carrying a perspective that centers on continued learning and growing?
- Do you mentally prepare yourself to perform your best every day—in school, work, practices, and competitions? Could you do better?
- Are you dwelling on the positives or the negatives?
- Are you remaining open to possibilities, to the creativity of the moment, and to the dynamics of the situation?
- Are you keeping a sense of joy in your pursuits?

Distraction Control

- Are you carrying a performance and life perspective that allows you to avoid, minimize, or control stress and distractions?
- Can you maintain your best focus even when faced with setbacks or distractions?

- Are you prepared to flow through distractions, refocus quickly, and regain control when faced with performance errors or setbacks? Can you do it consistently?
- Are you turning negatives into positives rather than positives into negatives?
- Do you have an effective plan for dealing with distractions?
- Are you acting on that plan? At every opportunity?

Ongoing Learning

- Are you committed to ongoing learning?
- Are you looking for the positives in yourself, others, and your performances?
- Are you drawing out relevant lessons from every performance and every important experience?
- Do you act on those lessons every day or at every opportunity— before your next performance, interaction, or event?
- Are you reflecting on the role that your mind-set and focus played in your interaction or performance?
- Do you act on those reflections? Consistently?

CHAPTER 2

A JOURNEY TO EXCELLENCE

My personal experiences as an athlete and performance-enhancement coach have been rich ones, bringing memorable highs that remain with me. Some involved achieving personal goals; others involved helping others achieve their goals; still others involved close human relationships and the sheer joy of being absorbed in the experience. I reached one of my achievement highs in sport when I first did a quadruple twisting back somersault on the trampoline. Some people were impressed. Others might say, "So what? Who cares if you can spin your body in the air four times before landing? What difference does it make?"

It may not make any difference to anyone else, but it made a difference to me. It felt great to accomplish something that required a commitment to extending my personal limits. Over a

WE WANT NOT ONLY TO LIVE, BUT TO HAVE SOMETHING TO LIVE FOR. FOR SOME OF US, THIS MEANS PURSUING OUR POTENTIAL THROUGH SPORT OR ANOTHER CHALLENGING PURSUIT.

period of about eight years, it began to happen bit by bit . . . half twist . . . full . . . double . . . triple . . . three and a half . . . three and three quarters . . . quadruple! A rush of excitement surged through my body . . . a satisfaction at having explored my potential in one small, seemingly meaningless but personally meaningful area of existence. I had stretched my personal limits.

The desire to become your personal best—to excel, to attain the highest standards of performance, to be supreme in your chosen field—is a worthy human pursuit that can lead to ongoing personal growth, a higher-level contribution to others and a more meaningful life. If none of us were concerned with the quality of our contributions, performance, work, creations, products, services, or interactions, our society would take a marked turn for the worse. Yet high levels of performance or excellence in any field do not come easily. The trail is often hard and steep. There are numerous obstacles to overcome and barriers to push aside. Becoming a highly skilled person in any field—sport, performing arts, medicine, science, business, writing, teaching, coaching, or parenting—demands a high level of commitment, an absorbing focus, and a belief in your own potential.

The greatest barriers in our pursuit of excellence are psychological barriers that we impose on ourselves, sometimes unknowingly. My failure to even attempt a quintuple somersault is a good example. Somehow I had come to believe that it was impossible. Perhaps it was like the 4-minute mile. At one time that, too, was viewed as an impossible barrier, until it was broken by one man— and then almost immediately by a host of others. It wasn't the physical makeup of runners that changed; it was their belief in what was possible. As your beliefs about limits change, your limits themselves change.

While traveling through Southeast Asia, I had the opportunity to see barefoot men walking across hot beds of coal. Those glowing embers generated incredible heat, yet the walkers emerged unblistered and unscarred. Is this unbelievable feat within the capacity of normal human beings? How many of us will ever call on this capacity? How many of us even believe that it is possible? Therein lie our limits. The firewalkers, and the world's best performers, are made of the same flesh and blood as you and I; it is their commitment and belief that are different. Therein lies their strength. Commitment and belief give birth to new realities.

Enjoying the Pursuit

Since I stopped competing in sport, I have had many joyful experiences in outdoor activities like trail running, canoeing, kayaking, and cross-country skiing. I never formally trained or competed in these activities, yet they continue to offer an abundance of challenges and joy.

One winter night, the sky was clear, the moon was full, and the night air crisp. The snow sparkled like dancing crystals under the moonlight. On this majestic evening, we set out to ski up a mountain trail to a small log chalet nestled among the trees. At the chalet we made a fire, had some wine and a bit of stew, and joked a little; then we headed back down the mountain. As I skied down, I became one with the mountain, not knowing where it ended and where I started. I felt so close to it, embracing it and feeling it hug me, as I flowed along that narrow snow-packed trail. I moved into shadows and out of shadows as the moonlight darted through the trees. I was totally absorbed in the experience. It was novel, challenging, sensual, fun, exciting, physically demanding, a meaningful trip with nature—a highlight experience, the kind that makes it feel so great to be alive. There are few contexts in which we have such close contact with other people, and ourselves, as we have in nature and sport.

Sport, nature, and other meaningful pursuits provide abundant opportunities to free ourselves for short periods to enjoy special moments not readily available elsewhere in society. We can live out our quest for excitement, personal control, or risk by deliberately accepting challenges that we then pursue with passion. Experiences like this make us feel more fully alive and more capable of directing our own destiny. This is one of the good reasons for seeking out meaningful challenges both within and outside of sport. Great satisfaction comes from embracing the experience, becoming competent, and feeling in control.

The continual process of seeking out and meeting challenges that are within our stretched capacity ensures that we continue to learn and grow. Delicious challenges that captivate us, absorb us, lift us, or stretch us in some meaningful way give heart to life and passion to our pursuits. What is delicious for me may not be for you. We each seek our own path, context, and level.

As a white-water canoeist I discovered that the challenge of running a river is not a conflict between human and nature, but rather a melding together of the two. You do not conquer a river, you experience it. The calculated risk, the momentary sense of meaning, and the intensity of the experience let you emerge feeling exhilarated and somehow better. This is a quest for self-fulfillment rather than a quest for victory over others or over the river. Many pursuits can be viewed in the same light. Each experience or exploration can lead to enjoyment, enlightenment, or discovery. There is no way to fail to experience the experience, and experiencing becomes the goal. The experience may lead to improved performance, self-discovery, personal satisfaction, and greater awareness, or it may simply be interesting, joyful, or meaningful in its own right.

This became clear while I paddled down the legendary South Nahanni river in the Canadian northwest territories. No one else can ever totally understand what that river meant to me, what it gave to me, or how we interacted along the way. So it is with the river of sport, performance, and life. No two people perceive things in the same way, even at the same instant. Each view is unique, each experience separate, each course different and irreplaceable . . . and so it should be.

Answering life's challenges in our own way is what provides personal meaning for each of us. Failure to respond to those challenges means falling short of our potential and abandoning the essence of life. In many prisoner of war camps, those who lacked the awareness of a meaning worth living for abandoned their will to live and curled up and died. Those who knew that a purpose or something of value awaited them survived the most incredible horrors and hardships. Suffering ceased to be suffering the moment it found meaning. Viktor Frankl, a young doctor who survived the horrors of imprisonment in a death camp, discovered through his experience that "striving to find meaning in one's life is the primary motivational force in man" (Frankl 1998, 154). It literally makes the difference between excellence and mediocrity, between life and death.

Although meaning for each of us is unique and changes over our lifetime, it flows most readily when we are connected to or striving toward some goal that we find worthy or feel is worthy of us. We can experience joy and meaning by committing ourselves to certain goals, ideals, or values; by experiencing someone or something of value to us; by being creative; or by choosing to do something for others, with others, or by ourselves, that we deem worthwhile. Sport and other high-performance pursuits are wonderful mediums for providing a sense of purpose and continuous challenge, as well as a range of intensity and emotion that is difficult to experience elsewhere. These pursuits can be rich and meaningful encounters if we approach them on our own terms. They offer numerous opportunities for personal growth and for stretching the limits of human potential, both physically and psychologically.

Personal excellence is a contest in which you must cooperate with yourself, drawing upon the natural reserves within your own mind and body, to develop your capabilities to the fullest. Each of us begins at a different departure point, mentally, physically, emotionally, and with respect to the support we are given. Look for the opportunities within each situation you face. Develop your own strengths. Make the most of what you have, whatever that may be. The true joy and challenge lies in pursuing ongoing personal growth, loving the pursuit, and living the various textures of your life.

ONE JOURNEY TO EXCELLENCE

I began working with Kerrin Lee Gartner when she was a 16-year-old on the Canadian women's Alpine ski team. Eight years later, at the Winter Olympics in Mirabel, France, Kerrin won the women's downhill on what was considered to be the fastest, most difficult women's race course ever. The following interview with Kerrin focuses on her path to personal excellence. I included her experiences here to illustrate how to act on the wheel of excellence in the real world of high-level performance. Perhaps it can serve as an inspiration or guide in your continued pursuit of personal excellence.

COMMITMENT

Terry: You have achieved the highest goal in downhill skiing, and you were able to do it in a very stressful situation. How would you describe your commitment to go after that goal?

Kerrin: The commitment is more than 100 percent. It's committed through the ups and downs. Committed through the good results and the bad results. Committed when you're coming in 50th and it looks like there's never an end to the bad results. You still have to be committed and still focused and still trying to win every race. I think the day that you let your commitment go is the day you don't have a chance to win.

Terry: How long did it take you to get ready for this one little run (the 1992 Olympic downhill)?

Kerrin: A lot of people assume it's an overnight success story. It's taken me nine years of hard work in international competition and many years before that. I think with all of your work, I think that shows how long it has taken me.

Terry: Over the last eight or nine years you've had lots of setbacks, lots of challenges to overcome, lots of injuries, and maybe some people not believing in you as much as you believed in yourself. How did you get yourself to keep going after your goals through some of those struggles?

Kerrin: The obvious struggles were my knee injuries, and each one took six months to about a year and a half to really recover from. It wasn't just the physical recovery. The mental recovery was the hardest part. There are always waves in life, and when you're down in ski racing, with a physical disability like my knees were, it was always important to keep my goals set, to always believe in myself, and to look at the

Being completely focused is the only way you can achieve your goal.

reasons why I was going through these struggles, to look at the end result really. I made little tiny goals for myself—little tiny steps, focused on little things. I stayed focused through every single bad thing, stayed focused, stayed focused, stayed focused. I think that's the only way through it, to go gradually and continue believing in yourself the whole way. That's the key to everything when you're down.

FOCUSED CONNECTION

Terry: When you talk about being focused in training, focused in races, can you describe what that is?

Kerrin: My very best focus is when everything happens naturally. I don't even think about it. A lot of people want to know exactly what I am thinking in certain parts of the course, or what I'm thinking in the start gate, or when I go through the finish. It's almost a feeling. The focus is so clear that you shut your thoughts off and you trust yourself and believe in yourself. You've already prepared for years. All you do is go; it's very natural. The focus is so crisp. You're so connected. That happened to me at the Olympics. There are so many words to describe it, there's autopilot, connection, tunnel vision, or just being 100 percent focused. It's all more of a feeling. It turns from thoughts into feelings and natural motions on skis. You don't really have any distinct thoughts when you're going down. You don't see the people on the side of the hill. You don't see anything. You're just naturally doing what you do.

CONFIDENCE

Terry: I am interested in how your confidence in your capacity has changed over the years. I know this year you really knew you could do it. How would you describe the strengthening of your belief?

Kerrin: Actually, it's amazing because people naturally assume you always believe in yourself from day one. When your results aren't there, the first thing that shatters is your belief and confidence. That's a key to success, and over the years I've developed belief in myself. I knew I could be on the podium, and I knew I would be a winner, but as much as I know and as much as I can believe, until it happens, 100 percent belief isn't there. I really talked myself into it this year. I knew I was skiing as well as anybody on the World Cup circuit. I've had top five results consistently in the last two years, and I really, really believed, with 110 percent of myself, that if there was a course that I had a chance to win on, it was the Olympic course. Just by believing in myself, and always talking to myself very positively, and putting positive thoughts in my mind, it only encouraged the belief I already had.

Terry: So how would you talk to yourself positively?

Kerrin: I would turn anything negative into a positive. If I had a bad run, I would take a positive out of it anyway. If I had a run where I was only good on half of it, I would take a positive and build on it. That made me believe in myself more each time I ran the course. Each time I did anything, I could build positive emotions on it. On race day at the Olympics, it was very flat light, very foggy, which is not very pleasant in downhill. The first positive thing I did was say to myself, *You're good in flat light; you're one of the best skiers in flat light. This is your opportunity right now; go for it!* I really am one of the better skiers in flat light. Although I don't like it any more than anyone else, I can still be aggressive and I can still ski like I want to ski.

Positive Images

Terry: Did you do much imagery in preparing for your Olympic race?

Kerrin: I've been doing imagery of the Olympics for about four years, but I started this course last February and have run it hundreds of times in my mind. So by the time I actually had the race day run, I had done it many times before. I just hadn't won it in reality yet!

Terry: What do you experience in your imagery of the race run?

Kerrin: I think a lot of people assume that imagery is pictures in your mind, and actually when I was 16, when we first started working together, it was very much like watching a videotape. I could watch anybody with my eyes closed and picture anybody skiing in a certain part of the course. It's advanced itself to the very special state where now it's more of a feeling. I can feel the feelings of skiing, and feel the motions. My thoughts almost turn into feeling. I think that is very important for athletes to do that in any sport.

Terry: What about imagery for getting through your injuries and back on track? Did you do anything there?

Kerrin: The first injury I had, I remember talking to you, and you said, "Remember to ski in your mind." I thought, "The last thing I want to do now is ski, because I'm injured." But I remember it didn't take me very long to get back on my skis in my mind. I skied [in my mind] basically every single day through my injury and through the recovery. It helped me keep my focus on what I was going through it for, and it made the pain and struggle a lot easier to take because I was still doing something very enjoyable in my head. Even if I was on crutches, in a cast, it made it a lot easier.

Terry: How did your first run go after those injuries?

Kerrin: I think by keeping my imagery there, it made it much simpler to get out on the downhill skis. In a real course, it made the speed adjustment much quicker. With the second injury, it just happened very naturally. I had already succeeded in being able to imagine myself skiing perfectly and I did it throughout the six months of recuperation. When I put my skis on, it was like I wasn't even off of them.

MENTAL READINESS

Terry: When you talk about mental readiness, what does that mean to you?

Kerrin: It means years of mental preparation. My first meeting with you was when I was 16 years old. I remember it very clearly. I was not very good at imagining myself skiing. I didn't understand why I even had to do it. Now it's come to a point where it's a part of my everyday life. If I'm hanging a picture in the living room, first I imagine where I want it, then I imagine how high I want it, and how far away from the wall.

I can see it all very clearly. Then I hang the picture, and it's in the right spot. That's a very simple example of what I can do when I ski, but when I ski I'm doing something danger-ous. I'm doing something that I want to do very badly. It's not worth making a mistake, so I have to use my imagina-tion and my imagery constantly throughout the whole year.

Terry: How did you approach your training runs for the Olympic downhill?

Kerrin: I just tried to stay very relaxed, work on certain parts of the course all week long, and kept my goals small. I worked on a 30-second section instead of the whole thing. That way I kept the pressure off myself as well. I didn't feel the need to win every single training run. I just felt the need to ski certain parts of the course well, and I think that was the key to a lot of it. It allowed me to stay relaxed. It kept the press away a little bit. The press didn't think I was a key person, even though I thought I was.

Terry: You skied each section well, but you picked different sec-tions to go after on different runs.

Kerrin: Yes. We only got to ski the top 30 seconds of the course twice, and that was where I had trouble at the beginning of the week. The last training run, I concentrated solely on the first 30 or 40 seconds, and then relaxed and basically just skied the rest. I still had a very good run, so I knew I was ready to do well.

Terry: What were your reminders going into the race?

Kerrin: Actually, I kept it pretty simple. I just had the reminder to just go for it, take the advantage, and I knew I had the chance to make it my day. I didn't want to risk not going for it and not taking the advantages. I was very relaxed, which was obviously a key to it all.

DISTRACTION CONTROL

Terry: The Olympic Games are a huge distraction for most athletes. How were you able to come through with a great run under the most distracting circumstances?

Kerrin: I've taken lessons from a lot of different races. One of the races I took a very valuable lesson from was the 1988 Olympics. I was very distracted in 1988. I wanted to win very badly. In preparing for 1992, what I did was take everything I learned, which included putting myself first, putting what I need first, and concentrating on what I needed to concentrate on in everyday races. I was very relaxed. I knew what my job was. All I had to do was go out and do it. Once I was on the chair lift in the morning, everything was fine. I took an hour or two to deal with all of the distractions in a one-block period. I left the rest of the time to myself. I think it's important to make sure that you're relaxed and ready to go. If you get too distracted, then you can't focus anyway, and you don't have a chance to win.

Terry: So you dealt with some of the people and media things and then had a time that you just clicked off to get away from it all?

Kerrin: Yes. Once I left the hill and the race site, which is where most of the stress and distractions are, I was on my own. It was like my normal everyday life—playing card games, reading books, and just staying relaxed. I remember in Calgary, all I did was think about the race all day long. In Mirabel I couldn't have been more relaxed.

Terry: What about on site? What perspective allowed you to focus on your performance instead of the outcome?

Kerrin: I had a very good teacher, Terry! I think I've learned, definitely, not to focus on the outcome of any event. Although you dream about it, and I dreamed about the gold medal for many years, I think the best thing for me is that I've learned to concentrate on what I need to concentrate on. I needed to concentrate on having a good warm-up in the morning, concentrate on being very smooth, very quick, looking for speed in the course. It carried right through to my race. I went to the start and I wasn't concentrating on the final result, I was concentrating on what I needed to do to ski my very best. It just became natural for me. I went through the same motions as I go through every race. It just happened naturally.

Terry: Were there any points where you had to refocus to get back on track within the race?

Kerrin: There was one, actually. It didn't show up too well on TV, but there was one spot where I caught my ski and it went out from underneath me. It really caught me off balance, and I remember my mind slipping away a bit there. It didn't take long to get it back. I just said *Come on* to myself. It's always been a key. It means everything that I can possibly think in one split second. I got right back together, and the bottom half of the course was exceptionally good.

Terry: A lot of athletes who win gold medals really struggle in their next races because of the expectations placed on them and the expectations they place on themselves. You had great races in your subsequent World Cups. How was your focus in those races?

Kerrin: Actually, I was very tired going into the first World Cup race after my Olympic win. I wasn't expecting much of myself. I went out in the morning, and my warm-up didn't go as planned. I didn't ski as well as I had hoped. I had been thinking a lot about the outcome. I realized it right away, and I changed my thought pattern by admitting it and by getting the focus into my mind that I really needed to focus on. I changed into the mode that works for me. I thought of going for it, being aggressive, and of all my key thoughts. When I was standing in the start gate I knew that I had an opportunity to win the race. I pushed out of the gate and went into my automatic pilot without thinking about anything other than my key thoughts. I just kept my focus. I was second by three one-hundredths, that's pretty close to winning. I was pretty happy with that result after everything that had happened.

Terry: If a negative thought or something that doesn't help you slips into your mind, what do you find is best for getting back on track?

Kerrin: When I notice myself thinking thoughts that I don't want to be thinking and don't work for me, or when I start thinking about the outcome or final result, I try to notice it first, and rectify it by thinking of things that work for me.

Terry: Has it taken a while to be able to get your thoughts working for you like that?

Kerrin: It's taken a long time. I remember races in the past where I wouldn't even realize why I had blown it in that race until a year later. Last year at a downhill in Lake Louise I had been doing very well, winning training runs. On race day, I came in fifth, and I realized after the race that my approach was wrong. I was thinking the wrong things. Now I've started to realize if I'm thinking the wrong things before I even race. This gives me a chance to have a good race before racing.

Terry: So you change your thinking, or your focus, before the race begins, to have a better chance at performing well?

Kerrin: Exactly. If I wake up and I realize my head is there, in the right place, I let my thought patterns work naturally and I have a good race. If it's not there or something distracts me in the start or warm-up in the morning, then I know my refocusing thoughts. I know what brings me back to my good results and good focus.

ONGOING LEARNING

Terry: Part of your ongoing evaluation plan is to pull out positive things from every performance to enhance your confidence or feel good, as well as to learn from the experience. Can you comment on that?

Kerrin: It's taken me many years to pull something out of each run. If I'm last in a race I've learned to still pull something out of it. Most times I give 110 percent effort and that's enough for me. If you try as hard as you can try and you give the effort you can give, you have to be satisfied with the result because you really couldn't have done more anyway. The lessons that I pulled out of the Olympics and applied to other World Cups afterwards were to stay relaxed and to concentrate on what I know works. There are certain key thoughts that work for me on race day, and most of it's just relaxing and going for it, counting on my natural instincts to take over. When that happens, I have my best races.

Terry: I've noticed over the past couple of years you are more willing to follow your own path, to do things that you know help you, even when some people may not agree. How has that unfolded?

Kerrin: I'm in an individual sport that is run in a team manner, so sometimes it's very hard to do things like an individual and to follow my own path. I've come to realize that I must trust myself 100 percent and believe in myself. When I need something a little bit different from what the rest of the girls need, I am willing to take a risk and go for that to get the win.

Terry: So now that you know what you need to perform your best or win, you are able to respect patterns and gain from them.

Kerrin: Exactly. You learn about yourself throughout your whole career. I've been out there for eight years and I've learned a lot. I've taken lessons from many different things. Now I can apply those lessons. At the Olympics, I knew I had to be away from the team and had to be on my own and away from the distractions of the village. I did that and it paid off.

Terry: Now that you have won the gold medal, there are lots of people wanting your time. How are you planning to respect your needs even though you have people tugging at you?

Kerrin: At first it was difficult because it was hard for me to say no. I wasn't used to being an Olympic champion or having that much attention. I've realized I really have to listen to my insides. I have to listen to what I feel, and when I'm run down and tired, I have to say no. I have to say, "I'm sorry, I can't do it tonight, or next week, or the week after; I need a couple of weeks off." I've realized it's OK to say no, and to look after myself first, because my career is not finished. I know I can still win out there.

Terry: It's better to listen to yourself and to your body and do something positive about it before you are totally exhausted, rather than after.

Kerrin: Exactly. I think you have to learn to do that as an athlete. You really have to learn to respect your body. Often you realize a week before it happens that you are getting close to being too tired, and you have to take a week off. It's very important to be able to listen to yourself and follow your feelings as well. If I think I need time off, it's very important that I take it off instead of listening to other people. Because if I don't believe I'm on the right program, then I won't win a race. I really have to believe in what I'm doing 100 percent. The program has to be right for me.

Terry: You had a very high commitment to ski racing, but you also seemed to maintain a commitment in your relationships with your family. How did you try to balance that?

Kerrin: I have a lot of support from my family, a lot of love in my family. I am from a large family of five children, and we were very close throughout my childhood. I think with the support that they gave me, it was very natural for me to put them number one. Although my career was ski racing, and that was very important to me, I think it's also important to keep my private life alive and separate. A lot of people were worried that when I got married my focus would be gone and I wouldn't be able to concentrate on winning a race. Surprisingly, it's done wonders for my skiing. It's made me relax, try hard, but know that it's not the end of the world if I don't win the race. Chances are I actually ski better.

MOST IMPORTANT MENTAL SKILLS

Terry: What mental skills or perspective do you think have helped you most in terms of pursuing your goals?

Kerrin: There are so many. I think they're all tied together. Obviously for skiing, imagery is very important as well as focusing. But no matter what you do and no matter how many things you practice, unless you believe in yourself, and have 100 percent confidence, you don't have a chance to succeed in anything. I think that's probably what got me through it, because if I didn't believe I could win a race, I probably would have quit years ago with my injuries. I just kept the belief and kept the focus.

Terry: What are the most important lessons that you learned from me?

Kerrin: Hmm! The most important lesson is probably always to learn something from everything that happens and apply it to the next event. To stay relaxed. I've taken a lot of lessons from every race I've had. I've learned a lot about myself and now I can be a lot more relaxed. My imagery is as clear as I could ever want it. I know exactly how to focus and I just know how to apply everything that I know how to do. I know how to apply it on race day.

SUGGESTIONS FOR ATHLETES AND OTHERS

Terry: What advice might you have for other people who are in pursuit of excellence?

Kerrin: From everything I've learned through ski racing, the first and foremost thing is you have to believe in yourself and what you've chosen to do. If you're a nurse, then you have to believe in yourself, and work as hard as you can to be a good nurse. No matter what profession you're in, I think if you try 100 percent to be as good as you can be, it doesn't matter how good you are as long as you believe within yourself that you've tried as hard as you can.

Terry: Are you applying the mental skills that you've been developing through your skiing to other areas of your life?

Kerrin: The mental skills I learned through ski racing come into play every single day, all the time. Learning to deal with distractions comes into play now with the press, or if you have an argument or a setback, it's learning to get through that. I have to deal with that and still get on with my life ... staying relaxed, taking the good points out, always taking something positive and still feeling good about yourself and about the situation. I think everything that I do in sport relates to real life. It relates to everybody's career. It really relates to everything. I think that's the key to it all. Once you're relaxed and confident upstairs in your mind, then everything else will follow. That's the key to it all.

PART II

COMMITTING TO EXCELLENCE

CHAPTER 3

COMMITMENT TO EXCELLENCE

Long before the Olympic Games, diver Sylvie Bernier, like many other Olympic champions, decided that she was going to win the Olympics. As the Games approached, she often dreamed of achieving her goal—in her own words, "like flashes all the time. Every day I would see myself doing perfect dives, walking down and getting the medal. When it actually happened, it felt like I had already done it before."

To achieve your potential, somewhere deep in your core you have to create the belief that you can do it. By dreaming about your big dream and focusing on your daily goals—the little steps—you nourish your commitment, your confidence, and your belief in your capacity.

Even if you never make it to your ultimate goal, your dream of getting there inspires you to be better than

MY GREATEST POWER IN LIFE IS MY POWER TO CHOOSE. I AM THE FINAL AUTHORITY OVER ME. I MAKE ME.

you otherwise would be. Great human accomplishments begin with some kind of vision or dream. Every great feat flashes in the mind before it surfaces as concrete reality, whether it be flying to the moon; becoming a great student, artist, or performer; making a difference to others; healing yourself; excelling in a relationship; or building a dynasty. Dreams precede reality; they nourish it, even create it.

Most often our dreams of excellence are reflections of the things we want to do, the ways we want to be, or places we want to go. Visions of excellence, of creative accomplishment, of harmonious relationships, are in themselves stimulating and fun; they provide direction and a lift of positive energy even if they do not always become absolute reality.

All the people with whom I have worked who have excelled at anything began with a dream of being their best, making a contribution, stretching their limits, or reaching the top. Think about your own dreams; nurture them in your mind, often. Go after your dreams; let them lead you. It's the only chance you have to move along your path of self-fulfillment and excellence.

STEPS TO EXCELLENCE

Why is it that two runners with identical physical capacities (percentage of fast- and slow-twitch muscle fiber, reaction time, limb size, aerobic capacity, and so on) run vastly different times? One becomes a world champion and the other a mediocre runner. Why do some athletes with all the right physical attributes never really excel? How do athletes with relatively little going for them physically meet world-class standards in extremely demanding events? The answer lies in using what one has to the fullest capacity.

Excellence is housed in a variety of shapes, sizes, colors, and cultures. Many great athletes emerge from highly systematic programs, but others come from countries that lack a real sports system. Personal excellence is largely a question of believing in your own capabilities and fully committing yourself to your own development.

I have interviewed some of the world's best athletes and coaches to get their views on the ingredients necessary to make it to the highest levels in their sports. Within each sport there was disagreement about the physical requirements necessary for excellence, but almost total agreement on the requisite psychological attributes. Commitment and focus were identified as the most essential keys to excellence. To excel in any field, you must become highly committed, and you also must develop the focus control required to perform your best under a variety of stressful circumstances.

Excellence in sport, school, relationships, the performing arts, and business begins with a dream or goal to which you bring commitment, intensity, and focus. At some point you have to say, *Hey, I want to be really good at this; I want this to work; I am going to do everything I can to be as good as I can be; I am making this a priority in my life.* To be your best, you must live this commitment and continue to stretch your current limits. Commitment alone doesn't guarantee success, but a lack of commitment guarantees that you'll fall short of your potential.

Michael Jordan (basketball); Wayne Gretzky (ice hockey); Tiger Woods (golf); Mia Hamm (soccer); and Olympic champions Larry Cain (canoeing), Kerrin Lee Gartner (downhill skiing), and Bonnie Blair (speed skating) are great examples of the kind of commitment

The focus and commitment Tiger Woods brings to his game make him the great player he is.

and focus required to become the best that one can be. Their commitment was reflected in the incredible intensity they brought to practice and competition. When they trained, they were there for a reason—to do their best and to accomplish their goals—and were focused every second out there. In competition, they were energized and superfocused. Nothing less than the best effort was enough. Their minds were on the right channel, and they were determined to perform their best—no matter what.

PERSONAL COMMITMENT

Your personal level of commitment is something you must work out for yourself. No one can tell you how important something is in your life; that is your decision. But it is clear that people who excel are extremely committed people. There is no way to achieve a high level of excellence without a high level of personal commitment.

At this point it might be useful for you to rate the importance of excelling in sport, or any other meaningful pursuit, on a scale from 1 to 10. A rating of 10 indicates that it is the most important thing in your life (high commitment), a 1 indicates it is not very important at all (low commitment), and a 5 indicates a middle position between the two.

> How important is it for you to excel in your sport (or other chosen pursuit)?
>
> **1**   **2**   **3**   **4**   **5**   **6**   **7**   **8**   **9**   **10**
> not very   the most important
> important   thing in my life

When a large group of marathon runners responded to this commitment scale, it became evident that those with the highest commitment (scores of 9 and 10) became the fastest runners. As the commitment scores decreased, the performance levels decreased proportionally. The same was true for performers in a variety of other pursuits.

When members of national teams were asked what the main difference was between them and others who did not make the national team, their response was "commitment" (for example, "wanting it more," and "being willing to train harder, smarter, or with more focus"). They sometimes stayed after practice, learned by watching others play or perform, practiced with more focus, and did extra when required. They were willing to make sacrifices, and they believed that they would one day be excellent performers. Perhaps most important was their commitment to be totally focused within the practice and performance arenas.

In a study with the National Hockey League (NHL), we interviewed top NHL coaches and scouts to learn what they saw as most important for a player to make it in the NHL (see p. 45). We asked them what they looked for when drafting a player into the NHL and why they thought that some players who were selected didn't make it. Commitment (desire, determination, attitude, heart, self-motivation) and focus were the crucial ingredients that tilted the balance between making it and not making it at the professional level. Making their hockey careers a top priority, maintaining personal pride, constantly trying to improve, and always investing maximum focus and effort were named as indicators of the kind of commitment necessary to succeed. The chief scout for one of the NHL's top teams expressed it as follows: "The main thing is that the player is willing to give that little extra when it's needed. . . . He's preparing himself to give that little bit more . . . even when he might be dead tired. . . . This separates the great hockey player from the good hockey player."

Physically talented athletes who do not make it in the major leagues are described as lacking in the area of commitment, focus, or distraction control (unable to cope with the stress of the pro situation on or off the field, court, or ice,—"could not cope with pro demands," "choked under pressure"). The difference between making it and not making it was highlighted in a discussion of the drafting of one of the NHL's most celebrated players—Bobby Clarke, former team captain and general manager of the Philadelphia Flyers hockey club.

> We drafted Bobby Clarke on our second round, but there was a boy we drafted on our first round who was bigger and stronger, could skate and shoot better than Clarke, but Clarke made it and he didn't. He never had the heart for the game. He wasn't willing to sacrifice that little bit extra that you need to be a professional hockey player. In practice, Clarke would be there 10 minutes longer and he would work harder. In a game, he got himself mentally prepared to give the extra . . . the other player didn't do that. Result—one went ahead, the other fell behind. Clarke did extra work on the ice,

where he had to give a little more to check the man, where he had to bear down. Where it showed more than any place is coming back. . . . Gotta give a little more. If you lose possession of the puck, now you have to dig down to your bootstraps for extra adrenaline to come back and check the man. Bobby Clarke would always show that. The other boy would put his head down and sort of give up. That's the difference between the two.

A commitment to do quality work is a prerequisite for excellence, but unless you also master the art of focus control you will continue to fall short of your goals or dreams. Excellence requires the development of strong, positive focusing skills, as well as an openness to learn from others.

A well-respected NHL coach who guided his team to several Stanley Cup championships offered some interesting advice in this regard:

- **Accept criticism.** "Our superstars can handle constructive criticism. . . .They can even handle unfair criticism. . . . If they make a mistake, they acknowledge it and do everything in their power to not make it again. . . . A person with star potential will not become a star if, when I criticize him or point out a mistake, he tries to fight me."

- **Don't be afraid to fail.** "If a superstar ever sees a slight opening, zip, he has the courage to go for the small hole. He won't hold back because he's afraid to fail."

- **Maintain composure.** "The best players maintain their composure . . .when there's a call that goes against them, maybe even a bad call. They stay cool, look to correct, and try to calm down the other players."

BEING YOUR BEST

To become the best you can possibly be, the first, most essential ingredient is your commitment to do the right things. It takes a commitment to train and rest your body so that you can perform under the most demanding conditions, and a commitment to train your mind to focus totally on executing your best performance skills under the most distracting circumstances.

Prerequisites for Excellence
(As Viewed by NHL Coaches and Scouts)

- Does constant work on the ice; is in on the action, always after the puck, the check, or the goal; makes things happen; gives a little extra when it is important.

- After a mistake, goal against, or coach's criticism, comes back with a strong shift, makes the right moves, stays in the play or game, and tries harder to correct or make up for the mistake.

- Never gives up (for example, takes a check, gets back into the play quickly, tries and tries again).

- Plans, evaluates, and corrects with line mates on the bench; encourages others; passes to better-positioned players on the ice.

- Takes tips, asks questions, listens, admits errors and corrects them without excuses; shows that he wants to learn.

- Pursues activities both in and out of season to maintain conditioning and improve skills (for example, fitness training, power skating).

- Learns how to perform in a big game as well as in a normal game; comes through in tight situations or close games; makes the big play when needed.

- Learns how to stay motivated, come back, and play well after a setback, mistake, missed chance, call against him or team, or bad penalty.

- Learns to control temper (for example, does not needlessly retaliate after a hit or setback). Learns to react to referee, coach, teammates, and fans in a mature and positive way, particularly in big games.

- Learns to adapt to the stress of success, travel, and playing with different players (for example, line switching) without negative effects on attitude or play.

- Learns to stay cool and confident under pressure (for example, is not moody and not a worrier; can maintain focus on getting the job done in pressure situations).

If you really want to become your best, acting on the following basic guidelines will help immensely:

• Set specific daily goals so that you know what you want to accomplish every day, every practice, or every work session. Before you begin, take some time to prepare mentally so that you get the most out of yourself during that practice or work session. Commit yourself to executing your skills with full focus. In practice sessions, simulate what you want to do in the performance setting. Run through complete, clean routines, programs, plays, or events on a regular basis. During work sessions, scrimmages, or run-throughs, focus 100 percent, every step of the way. Positive imagery is a way of programming your mind and body to perform closer to your potential. Imagine yourself successfully executing the skills you are trying to perfect.

• When preparing for an important competition, rest well, listen to your body, and avoid overworking or overtraining so that you go in rested, strong, and healthy. The commitment to rest well is as important as the commitment to train well. Without proper rest, the mind-body system falters and eventually breaks down. Discover what focus works bests for you. Where is your focus when you perform best? Respect this focus. Remind yourself to follow it in preparation sessions and during performances.

• Commit yourself to remaining positive. Practice overcoming distractions on a daily basis. Avoid wasting energy on things beyond your control. This will lead to higher-quality training, better performances, and more joyful living. Before important events, remind yourself of the focus that works best for you. Mentally prepare yourself to connect fully with your task for the entire performance, and remain focused through the distractions. Follow the pre-event preparation patterns that have resulted in your best performances. Imagine and feel yourself executing your perfect performance. This will ensure that the best performance program is fresh in your mind and body. Then close off your thinking and connect totally with your performance. Draw the lessons out of every event. What went well? What needs refining? Were you able to maintain your best focus for the whole performance? What do you want to do in the same way next time? What changes might be helpful? How do you want to approach your next performance, event, or competition? What reminders might help? Make a note of these key points and work on them so that you are even better prepared, mentally and physically, for your next challenge.

CHAPTER 4

FOCUSED CONNECTION TO GOALS

One night as I was driving down a little dirt road in the countryside near my home, something darted out of the darkness onto the road in front of me. My heart pounded as I lurched for the brakes. A large rust-colored cat was in pursuit of a little gray field mouse. The cat focused on that mouse as if nothing else in the world existed, as if some kind of radiant energy beam connected the cat to the mouse. If I had not hit the brakes, I would have run over the cat—but she pursued that mouse as if I didn't exist. Only after she had the mouse firmly clenched in her teeth did she acknowledge my existence and saunter off into the woods. This is an example of full focusing, the uninterrupted connection between two things: a cat and a mouse, a performer and his performance, an athlete and her goal.

WHERE YOUR MIND GOES, EVERYTHING FOLLOWS.

Did you ever observe a young child at play? If you watch a toddler playing, you will notice that the only thing that exists in his world at that time is the action or movement he is engaged in at that moment. He is totally unhindered by the chaos around him. The intensity of his focus is very similar to the connection of the cat with the mouse, or a great performer with his performance. If you could focus so completely as a child, you are capable of doing it more often now.

Let's suppose that the cat began to worry about being judged on her form as she stalked the mouse: Do you think the complete connection would remain? If, while a two-year-old child was playing, she began to worry about being assessed on her movements by all the big people around her, do you think the focus flow would remain, or be broken?

A 14-year-old competitive figure skater came to see me a few years ago precisely because she had lost this focused connection. She had entered her first major competition when she was 11 years old. At that time, she just went out and let it happen. She skated in the same way that very young children play, totally absorbed in her performance and oblivious to the outside world. It was only later, when she started to think about judges, other skaters, the audience, and evaluation, that she started getting uptight: "When people said I was expected to win, the feeling of pressure started." Her thoughts began to drift to others' expectations of her. She began to worry about her performance and about how it would affect her acceptance by others. That is when her anxiety began to rise and her performance began to slide. That is when she lost her focus—her natural connection.

As she attempted to regain this connection, what worked best for her was to try to re-create the focus and feelings that she had taken into her sport in her earlier years, to focus only on her own performance and forget about everything else.

When you free yourself from dwelling on outside pressures or expectations, when you are focused on the step in front of you and know that you will continue to be a valuable human being regardless of numerical outcomes, worry is less likely to intrude on and disrupt your performance or your life. This is when your focus is free to flow naturally. Worry is one of the greatest inhibitors of skilled performance. If you can learn to view performance opportunities or competition in a less worried way, or if you can focus in a way that is more absorbing than the worry, you will be well on your way to consistent performance at your optimum level.

A great example of the need to focus fully was shared in an interview I did with Chris Hadfield, former fighter pilot, test pilot, and top-notch astronaut.

> When you're flying an airplane at 500 miles an hour, there's all kinds of things that don't matter, and there's a few things that really, really matter. What's in front of you for the next kilometer really matters because you're going to be there in a few seconds. The whole rest of your world doesn't matter; what's going on with your car or at home, or what just happened 30 seconds ago, or whatever. What really matters is what's going to have the biggest impact on you in the next 30 seconds. In a high-performance airplane things happen quickly, especially when you're flying down low or flying with another aircraft. So you need to completely compartmentalize, and just be ready to disregard things that don't matter and worry about them later. Even though it may be life or death later, for now it doesn't matter and you can't pay attention to it. You need to focus on what is in front of you right now.
>
> When we docked with the Russian space station, of course, it was very focused and a lot of people were working real hard, especially with the problems we'd had in sorting out the real time ranging and such. We had a video camera running on the flight deck and I watched the video afterwards and all of us are working hard, scrambling, and we get ourselves docked and then we're running the mechanics and no one says a word. And it's probably five minutes later that one of the guys turns around and says, "Hey, we did it! Five minutes!" Because we were so focused on task-specific things that absolutely had to be done or it wouldn't succeed. There are times when if you don't focus right down to the critical items right there, you don't give yourself a chance. So you've got to learn to put things into their boxes and drawers and compartments to be able to succeed.
>
> I think I learned to focus that way incrementally over my whole life. I was a downhill ski racer as a teenager, and there's a lot of it in that. I grew up on a farm working with large machinery, and when you're moving something along that's big and heavy you need to be right with your machine, right there. It's an extension of your body. In downhill racing, you have the next 30 seconds to do it right—either you're getting a medal or you're falling and maybe breaking your leg. So that's a good opportunity to focus.

You can begin by doing it on a very small scale. Focus for this length of time to get something done that's difficult. Challenge yourself to do something that you can just barely do, and then learn how to focus on it until you can do it well. Then slowly expand that. We start flying a glider, then a piper cub, and then something a little bigger, and a twin, then a small jet, then a big jet, and then a space shuttle. That's all the same idea of training yourself and developing the skill set, and the confidence, and the ability, to focus and strip away irrelevant things. No matter what your field of study is, that same idea applies.

FOCUSING IN SPORT

When you are focused in sport, you are totally connected to what you are engaged in to the exclusion of everything else. In a very real sense, you and your performance become one, and nothing else in the world exists for that period of time.

In individual sports, best performances occur when athletes are totally connected or riveted to their performance, often to the point of performing on autopilot and letting their bodies lead without interference. In team sports, best performances likewise occur when players are totally focused and absorbed in the crucial aspects of their performance. They are totally aware of the flow of relevant play around them, completely trusting in their capacity to automatically read and react to that awareness, and totally connected to the execution of their own moves. Their focus must be readily adaptable, like the zoom lens on a camera, capable of zooming in and zooming out. For example, a point guard in basketball or a quarterback in football needs a wide-angle perspective when focused on reading the field for an open player, then a zooming in on the open player and an inner connection with making a crisp, accurate pass. The ideal performance focus is total connection to your performance in spite of the constantly changing demands of the performance.

It is important for you to discover which focus works best for you and under which specific circumstances. Initially you may experience this special kind of connection for only short periods. Work on allowing this focus to become a natural part of all of your performances.

Focusing on a goal requires you to connect with every fiber of your being.

Your best focus may sometimes feel like a nonfocus because you are letting a performance program unfold automatically—free from conscious thoughts, directives, or self-evaluation. Often, focusing just means tuning in to your body or remaining connected to your task. A lot of focusing practice involves learning to stay connected to what you are doing; discovering the feelings that free you to perform flawlessly; not letting irrelevant or distracting thoughts interfere with the natural performance program in your mind and body; trusting your body to do what it's been trained to do without forcing; and directing your mind or body when it begins to tire or deviate from an efficient performance program.

To improve your focusing skills and make them more consistent, set some goals to allow your best focus to surface more regularly. Here are seven practice tips that will help.

1. Use your imagination to feel yourself execute desired skills, programs, plays, or performances in your mind and body; then do those skills, letting them unfold naturally, without thought.

2. When you practice skills, focus on being totally connected to your moves.

3. If your sport or performance domain requires an awareness of other players or opponents you must react to, practice being aware of everything that is going on around you, then totally connect to your target.

4. Free yourself to execute your own moves without evaluation. Just let go and see what happens. Go by feel. Go by instinct. Free yourself to flow naturally.

5. In training and performance situations, try to recreate the mental and physical conditions that allow you to experience the feelings and focus associated with your best performances.

6. Use meaningful reminders to enter the state of mind that allows your best performance focus.

7. Work on holding that best focus for short periods, and try to gradually increase the time you are fully connected. The ultimate goal is to be able to hold that best focus, that total connection, throughout your entire performance every move, every step, or every stroke of the way.

HITTING YOUR TARGET

The goal of a world-class archer is to hit the center of the target with each arrow shot. He trains himself to find the middle of the middle, to see only one center. "In this state of full focus, he could be anywhere in the world and remain undistracted. He shoots each arrow as a separate entity, concentrating fully for the short period required to release that shot. The periods between are times to relax in which all tension, muscular and mental, is dissipated and the mind is freed from the last arrow in preparation for the next one-arrow effort" (Genge 1976).

One world champion archer described focusing as "blocking out everything in my world, except me and my target. The bow becomes an extension of me. All attention is focused on lining up my pin [sight] with the center of the target. At this point in time, that is all I see, hear, or feel. With the bow drawn and sight on target, a quick body scan can tell me if anything is off. If everything feels right, I hold focus and simply let the arrow fly. It will find the target. If something feels off, I lower the bow and draw again."

Once a person has trained her muscles and nervous system to shoot an arrow into the middle of a target, theoretically she should be able to put it into the center every time. What prevents her from doing this? Fatigue? Sometimes—but not on the first few rounds. Wind? Sometimes—but not on a calm day. What then? Like most other performers, archers are prevented from achieving their true potential by worry, distracting thoughts, and a loss of that totally connected focus with the target. They have the program in their mind and body to perform the skill flawlessly. They can do it without thinking. Their challenge, like yours, is to free the body and mind to connect totally with the goal—consistently.

What the world's best performers seek, and perfect, is a fully connected focus. The mind is cleared of irrelevant thoughts, and the focus is centered only on what is important at that moment. Outside distractions and unwanted tension are absent. The focus is centered on a specific target—first the preparation, then the doing—a total connection with one's own body or performance.

Developing your ability to fully connect with the important little steps in your performance, and hold it there, is critical to consistent high-level performance. Full focusing is a learned skill that must be practiced to be perfected. Here are some general focusing exercises that you can try:

OUTSIDE YOUR PERFORMANCE SETTING

Try the following to help you focus on your goals.

• When you are sitting in a classroom or listening to someone speak, try to clear your mind of everything else and connect fully with what that person is saying. See how long you can hold that connected focus.

• Practice fully focusing only on what you are doing, with other people watching or talking—for example, while you are reading, studying, hammering nails, or performing. Relax, then focus fully.

• Scan the page that is in front of you now. Pick the last three words in this sentence and focus on them. Focus on these words until they stand out more than anything else on the page. Then back up your focus so that you become aware of the sentence. Now pick the word focus, and let yourself become more aware of it than others around it. Good!

• See how it feels to focus on different kinds of thoughts or feelings. Have a run today, and as you extend your leg, think *stretch* or *float*. Do this about 10 times in a row. See what happens. Then try thinking *power* when your left foot hits the ground, and again when your right foot touches the ground. Do this about 10 times in a row. See what happens.

• Do some body scans. Focus on the sensations in different parts of your body. How do the soles of your feet feel right now as you sit here reading? Are they warm? Where is the feeling centered? Are your calves relaxed? What does your behind feel like right now? Tune into that feeling. Does it feel weighted down? Is it relaxed? Is it warm? Is there a feeling of pressure? Lift up one cheek, then the other. Does that feel better? I thought it might. Do it again. Now focus on your shoulders. Are they relaxed? Let them drop a little. Think relaxation into your shoulders. Wiggle them a bit. Roll your head. Relax. That's better.

• Sit quietly, relax your breathing, and focus on looking at something in front of you like a table, a pen, an insect, a flower, a painting, a piece of fruit, a leaf, the bark of a tree, a friend's hand or face, a cloud. Really focus on it; look closely at its shape, texture, design, and feel; get absorbed in it.

• Sit quietly, let yourself relax, and focus on listening to something like the voices of birds, the wind, the leaves, or other sounds that you hear around you right now. Get absorbed in one of those sounds; then let it fade away by absorbing yourself in another sound or another focus.

• Line up several targets or objects. Become aware of all the targets. Then begin to narrow your focus until you are aware of only one target, then the center of that target, then the center of the center of the target. Let all other visions blur into the background; let all external sounds become inaudible. Connect fully with that target.

• Close your eyes and focus on a specific positive thought, repeat it to yourself, then stop thinking for about five breaths, then refocus on the specific positive thought.

Inside Your Performance Setting

These suggestions may help you focus within your performance setting.

• Stand quietly, let your shoulders relax, and think about doing a particular skill or movement. Try to imagine and feel the perfect execution of that skill. Then do the skill, letting your body perform automatically.

• Seek the feel of the movement. If the feel is right, everything else will be right.

• When you are feeling stressed, try slowing everything down. . . . Move slowly, talk slowly, stretch slowly; breathe in a slow, deep, and relaxed way.

• When you are distracted, try clearing the distractions from your mind by thinking about the little things you have to do to perform your best. Everything else is unimportant.

• After making an error, breathe, clear your mind, and shift your focus to doing what will help you execute the next skill correctly. Get good at doing this.

• Prepare yourself to focus in the moment—on one shot, one stroke, one swing, one step at a time, disregarding past and future. Remind yourself to seek this connected focus every day.

• Use simple reminders (for example, *connect, focus, smooth, relax, be here*) to keep your mind on target. Find a good image or reminder that will guide you back into your best connected focus.

• Embrace the joy in your pursuit.

If you experience problems with maintaining your focus, relax your body, relax your focus, lighten your load, try easier, without forcing it. Liken your efforts to this ancient Chinese saying: "Sitting quietly, doing nothing, spring comes, the grass grows by itself." A calm mind reflects the clearest focus just as a tranquil lake casts the clearest reflection. A single focus or vision that fully absorbs your awareness frees your body to follow the visions of your mind.

The world's top performers achieve their best results when they connect fully with their performances and clear their minds of thoughts about outcome. This focus is reflected clearly by this statement by an Olympic athlete: "For my best performances, I'm thinking about how to shoot correctly, letting shooting sequences run through my head . . . seeing myself in control, confident. It is very important for me not to start adding the score and projecting what the score might be. If during the last few ends I become nervous and start to worry about blowing it, I have to work hard to keep my shooting sequence in mind *(form, form, form)* and not the glory of shooting a high score."

Another top Olympic athlete maintains, "I'm not nervous in a negative sense in advance, because I remain who I am, myself, so that it is impossible for other competitors to have a harmful effect on me." She doesn't go through a big comparison scene, worrying about how well others are performing. She simply does her own thing. "For my best performances, I empty my mind and I feel as though it isn't me performing, but at the same time I feel totally connected with the feelings in my body. It's as if my subconscious is doing the performance. I imagine the perfect movement in my head, and the rest follows automatically." After the event, she evaluates why her performance was good or bad. If it was good, she asks herself, *How did I get my mind working that way, so I can duplicate it the next time?* If her performance was not up to par, she draws out the lessons and moves on. In her own words, "I probably work harder and learn more when something goes wrong."

The difference between best and worst performances lies within your own thoughts and focus. In poor performances, you allow negative or distracting thoughts (about other performers, your weaknesses, others' expectations, fatigue, a bad warm-up or mistake, the weather, or final placing) to interfere with a fully connected focus. In best performances, you are able to stay in the moment, which is the only one that you can influence anyway. If you find yourself losing your best focus, these strategies may help you regain it.

FOCUSING STRATEGIES

Find your best focus by trying one of the following suggestions.

- Return to basics; follow your game plan.
- Focus only on your target or the immediate step in front of you.
- Reassure yourself that you have trained and are ready (for example, *I have done this skill a thousand times before—I am fully capable of doing it well*).
- Remind yourself of your past best performances and recall the feelings and focus associated with them.
- Remember that your goals are realistic—all you want to do is to perform as you are capable of performing.
- Focus on doing what is right for you rather than worrying about what is wrong.

- Imagine the perfect execution of your skills, then do what you are fully capable of doing.
- Remind yourself to stay in the moment. Forget the past, the other athletes or performers, the final score. Focus on doing your job.
- Rivet your focus on the little steps.
- Remind yourself that it's just another game or performance.
- Do a careful postperformance analysis of good and bad performances. It is invaluable, even two or three days afterward.
- Training and performing should be enjoyed. Embrace the good parts. If you hate it, leave it.

No Worries

Did you ever wonder why we spend time worrying when all it does is interfere with our own effectiveness?

Worry creates stress, drains energy, and takes us away from our best performance focus. To close the door on unproductive worry, you can shift your focus to concrete actions that help prepare you to do something constructive or connect you to your performance. Many performers find that once they are actively engaged in something that absorbs them, such as a preperformance routine or the game itself, the worry leaves. This is because they have successfully shifted their focus away from worry to another absorbing focus. If your focus is centered on something other than worry, you cannot be worrying at the same time.

You can learn to shift your focus away from worry by refocusing on something else that you would prefer to be doing, the specific strategy or technique to be followed, your game plan, positive images, or relaxed breathing. This shift in focus will help you to stop comparing yourself, doubting yourself, or worrying about what is at this moment beyond your control. The goal is to stop evaluating yourself, putting yourself down, or projecting into the future, and instead to support yourself or completely absorb yourself in the process of doing what you want to do.

When attempting to shift focus, let your focus absorb itself in what you want to do next. For example, let your focus shift from self-condemnation over the past to absorption in the present. If you practice this often in a variety of settings, you will definitely increase your effectiveness.

Before reading the next chapter, close your eyes for a minute and let yourself relax. When you open your eyes, get up, stretch, and feel refreshed, so that you can really focus on what you are about to read in the next chapter, or really connect with whatever you plan to do next. Remember to embrace the simple moments and joys in your life.

CHAPTER 5

MEANINGFUL GOALS

I've had frustrated athletes and students come to me and say that they can't seem to meet their goals. Some discussions go something like this:

> Me: Did you set specific goals for yourself?
>
> Student: Oh, yes—I tried it and it didn't work, so I stopped setting goals.
>
> Me: What were your goals?
>
> Student: To compete in the Olympics. (Or "To finish my thesis by the summer," "To get an A in your class"; you get the idea.)
>
> Me: Oh, I see. Did you set short-term goals, every day, that were totally within your control . . . like what you are going to do today, in the next hour, that will bring you one step closer to being your best?

A JOURNEY OF A LIFETIME BEGINS WITH A SINGLE VISION— FOLLOWED BY ONE STEP, THEN ANOTHER AND ANOTHER.

Student: No, not really.

Me: Do you have any specific goals for tomorrow?

Student: No.

It's not unusual for people to set only long-term, far-off goals without focusing enough on the present. It is the present that gets us to the future in the way we wish to get there. Long-term goals can help motivate and guide you, but you also need lots of little daily goals that take you progressively to your desired destination. In your journey to personal excellence, it is best to focus most of your energy on taking little steps that are within your control—to improve your skills, your preparation, your execution, your routines—and to be the best you can be that day. Many outcomes in competitive situations are not within your direct control because you do not control competitors, teammates, judges, officials, playing conditions, or the weather—all of which can influence outcomes. When you set goals that require control over elements that are beyond your control, you set yourself up for frustration and needless anxiety. It is challenging enough to control what is within your control—your own focus and your own best performance.

EVERYDAY GOALS

For goal setting to be most effective, set specific, relevant, daily goals, then absorb yourself in pursuing them. Encourage yourself, compliment yourself, and enjoy yourself as you achieve each short-term goal and move toward long-term ones. You want to get from point A to point B as efficiently and joyfully as possible, and this process of focusing on the little steps gets you there. Let's say that you want to become the best performer you can be, or that you want to write a book. Great! What are you going to do about it in the next five minutes, hour, day, week, month, year? Setting specific daily goals and pursuing them in a systematic and focused way separates those who want to meet challenges and excel from those who actually do.

Let's take the writing of this book as an example. I could simply write as often as I feel like it and finish whenever the book is complete (if ever). Or I could set some concrete goals for myself, saying that I want to finish this section today, before eating supper; write the following section by the end of the week; finish the next chapter by the end of the month; complete the book by the end of the summer. I've tried the "do it when I feel like it" approach, and it never seems to advance me very quickly toward my goal. But when I set very specific short-term and long-term goals for myself, things begin to happen.

For me, the process goes something like this. First, I think about whether completing the book is important to me. This is a critical first step, because only if I am committed to the goal do I have a realistic chance of achieving it with quality. I decide that this goal is an important one for me because I like writing, creating, and reflecting; and I want to share my thoughts with others in hopes of helping them to achieve some of their goals. Sharing meaningful thoughts and helping others makes me feel worthy. Also, I love to see a bunch of visions become a bunch of roughly typed pages and then become a real live book. It's very concrete: I can see what I'm accomplishing, and I can touch it, much as in sport.

The concreteness of progress in most sports is readily obvious. New tricks, better technique, faster times, higher jumps, better plays, improved rankings—all can be seen and felt. You know exactly where you are, and you can see progress in a way that is often not possible in other aspects of life. When I teach a class, for example, it is very difficult to know whether I've really accomplished anything. I'm often not left with anything concrete that tells me where I am, where the students are, or whether I have effected any real change. Sport and some of the performing arts, on the other hand, offer indisputable proof of progress, which can yield much personal meaning and add joy to life.

Back to my example of writing this book. Because I have determined at the outset that this is important to me, I begin to set some goals that I think are realistic in terms of my time, abilities, and motivation. Just the process of thinking about specific goals gets my mind moving. When my goals and projected completion dates are written down on paper, that helps even more. At this moment I'm just a little behind in meeting my goals—but they were somewhat ambitious. Some things took slightly longer to refine than expected. There was no reason to panic; I simply readjusted the goals to bring them in line with reality. At times I move ahead of my stated goals, usually when things seem to flow just right. Some days I really need a break from writing. I take that break because it allows me to return refreshed. The next day I usually work twice as well—particularly if I know that my goal is to complete a certain amount by the end of the week.

I get a great feeling of satisfaction from fulfilling my own goals. It makes me feel alive and worthy. It shows me that I can decide to do something that is important to me, and then do it. That feels good, even if the goal is only a short-term one. Often this feeling is enough to keep me moving toward the next goal, as long as I feel the goal is a worthy one. Sometimes I tell myself that I am pleased with myself . . . and I mean it! If the goal has been difficult to meet or if I'm tired or need a lift, I take a few days off, go to nature, spend time with my family or friends, ski, kayak, see a movie, or just relax. I treat myself well when I think I need or deserve a treat. We all need and deserve that.

Once you decide that something is worth pursuing, you can apply these same mental skills to reach a high level in virtually any area of life. Whether you want to improve your focus; win a championship; excel in school, business, or the performing arts; run for your health; improve a relationship; or balance your life, the basic procedures are the same. You need commitment, focus, a positive mind-set, and specific goals that are relevant to your pursuit.

Reach greater heights with positive thinking and specific goals.

Short-Term and Long-Term Goals

Your coach or a respected veteran performer may be able to assist you in establishing realistic but challenging goals by helping you translate your overall aims into specific actions, moves, plays, times, programs, routines, scores, or performance requirements. Establish a series of short-term goals, with specific target dates for achievement, that relate to your long-term goals. Achieving a goal, even a short-term one, makes you feel competent and inspires you to pursue your next goal, thereby helping you to maintain commitment and build self-confidence.

Short-term goals might include mastering a certain skill, doing quality work, getting adequate rest, or completing a certain number of programs or assignments—today, by the end of the week, by the end of the month. Your short-term goals can help you improve not only physically, but mentally; thus it's important to set goals for focusing, mental imagery, relaxation, positive thinking, distraction control, and drawing out lessons from your experiences.

Long-term goals may include improving your overall attitude or mental game; excelling in your performance domain; mastering a particular routine or program; deciding on the speed, distance, time, or performance level you want to attain by the end of this year and in the following year; or achieving a personal best in an important assignment, performance, or competition.

If you can write down your goals in concrete terms (I will accomplish this by this time) you have a greater chance of accomplishing your objectives, and in less time than you otherwise would. How many preparation days are left before your next performance, presentation, trials, audition, assignment, championship, or most important goal? Write down your goals and the number of days remaining before your next key event. It is often enough to stimulate some positive action.

Many top performers keep daily training logs or performance diaries to direct and monitor their own progress. By listing goals set and met, recording training programs, and noting mental factors associated with best and less than best practices and performances, you can speed up your progress and learn more from your experiences.

Think about tomorrow's goals tonight before you go to sleep or in the morning before you get out of bed. Just lie there for a few minutes and run through your mind what you want to accomplish today. This sets the stage for doing the good things you want to do every day.

It is important that you set your own goals, rather than having someone else set them for you. When you make the decision, it increases your commitment to that goal. Shared goal setting—for example, between you and your coach or supervisor, you and your parents, or you and your partner—is valuable as long as you have personally weighed the situation and feel that the goal is what you really want.

For most people, identifying their own goals and having ample input into their preparation program is the most effective means for reaching their potential. I know that this is true for most high-performance athletes, and it's also true for me. I know better than anyone else what I have done and what I want to do. I also know better than others what will help me and what I need at a particular moment.

Input from others is extremely important and can be very meaningful if it is constructive and on target. Still, you are a unique individual. No one else is exactly like you. If you are to become your best, you and those around you must respect your unique qualities and your differences. It is often those differences that lead to greatness.

Pursuing meaningful goals helps you to know yourself better, to extend yourself farther, and to give what you are capable of giving to yourself and to others. If you really want to explore and embrace your own potential, set individualized goals. They will likely become less formal as you become more experienced with the process, but they will still be there in your mind and will continue to guide you.

MOVING TOWARD YOUR GOALS

Excellence in any field depends largely on

- knowing where you want to go (having a vision),
- how much you really want to get there (commitment),
- how strongly you believe in your ability to arrive at your desired destination (believing in your capacity), and
- connecting with the step in front of you (focused connection).

Your performance is a function of your visions and expectations for yourself. If you see yourself as having something of value to offer, as having a contribution to make, as having a lot of potential, then you will act accordingly. If you view yourself as having little or nothing to offer, then this will likewise be reflected in your performance. Don't sell yourself short! You have a whole lot more to offer than most people recognize. How can I say that? I don't even know you, right? Well, if you are anything like other members of the human species whom I have encountered, you have all kinds of untapped potential. And if you have picked up a book like this, you probably have visions of realizing some of that potential.

I once worked with a cross-country skier who was overflowing with natural talent. However, he didn't think he could be a great athlete because he had no "proof"; that was what he wanted in order to believe in himself. One way of providing this proof that can boost your confidence in your potential is to chart your progress systematically so that you can see your improvement. Another way is to work, train, or compete with some highly respected performers so you realize that they are human too and that you can hang in there with them at least for certain assignments or parts of training or competition. Start looking for the good things in yourself and in your performances instead of always looking for what is bad. Remind yourself of what you do well and give yourself suggestions for improvement in a positive and constructive manner. Walk out there and try being totally positive with yourself. You will feel better, work better, and perform better; and it might even rub off on those around you who you care about.

We all start with one constant: There are 24 hours in a day! If I'm training or working toward a specific goal, I might as well dig in and do as much quality work as I can during the time I'm there. If I mentally prepare myself to complete every task as efficiently as I can, with the highest quality of focus and effort, I can meet my goals and still have time for myself, my family, and my friends. By organizing your time—planning your work or workout and setting specific daily goals—you can accomplish more with quality while you are working or training and still leave time for adequate rest and other joys in life. You can even schedule some relaxation time, some fun time, some free time.

Three of my students observed some local gymnasts at practice. What they recorded was the actual time each gymnast spent performing on the apparatus during a 2-hour workout. The average time was about 15 minutes. How much time do you spend committed to focused, high-quality training or work during a practice or work session? Could you be using your time more effectively? Probably. But you have to be careful not to go overboard in the other direction. You can't be pushing your limits every second. You need time to breathe, to reflect, to evaluate previous performances, to mentally prepare for a high-quality effort, to rest, to interact with others, and sometimes to have fun.

I guess it all boils down to what you want at different stages, and within different components of your life. If it doesn't really matter to you whether you use your time more efficiently or whether you improve much in a particular area—forget the performance charts and the striving for excellence, and focus on getting what you want out of the experience . . . fun, fitness, social interaction, the wind and sun on your face, or whatever you are seeking. There is absolutely nothing wrong with making that decision. But if you want to excel in a particular field, then a major commitment is required.

When making this kind of commitment, it helps to be quite sure that the goal, and the overall process of striving to reach it, is important enough to you to warrant your commitment. Often we know intuitively whether something is worth pursuing with commitment. Other times it is helpful to ask ourselves some questions or discuss our feelings with the people closest to us. If you think about each of the following questions and respond to them honestly (perhaps in writing), the issue will be clearer in your own mind, and you should be in a better position to make a decision that is right for you. If you decide to pursue this path with commitment, think about the following:

- Are you doing it because you really want to do it, or because someone else wants you to do it?
- Is this something in which you can find ongoing joy and satisfaction?
- Why do you want to do this?
- What do you expect to gain?
- What do you expect to lose?
- Do you think it's really worth the effort when there are no guarantees of the final outcome?

When you recognize that you do have a choice, and you make a conscious decision in either direction, you can often approach things in a more positive light. If the decision is to "go for it" and you are dedicated to this choice, you will have a greater capacity to endure the demands that follow. It was Friedrich Nietzsche who wrote that "he who has a reason why can bear with almost any how." If your decision is to "let it go," then you are free to pursue other, perhaps more meaningful, pursuits.

You can sometimes bolster your commitment to a goal by talking with family members, fellow performers, coaches, or friends about your decision or mission. Some athletes go so far as to make a public statement about their goals in an attempt to increase their commitment to pursue them. Most of us do not gain from making our goals public, but we can all gain from the support and encouragement of important people in our lives as we attempt to pursue our personal goals.

When goals set clash with goals met, it is helpful to remember that unmet goals, plateaus, times of seemingly little or no progress, and even periods of backsliding are natural, and that everyone faces these experiences at some point. Progress is a series of ups and downs; it is by no means all clear sailing. Even when you see no obvious signs of improvement, you may still be laying the groundwork for future progress. Think of the best performer in your discipline: He has also been discouraged. She has also had problems to overcome and goals she has not met. But somehow that person persists and overcomes the obstacles. That is part of the *path to excellence.* It is also part of the path of day-to-day living.

It's no tragedy to fall short of a particular goal. You grow from the experience, learn from it, adjust your goal, stick some short-term goals or intermediate steps in front of it. A temporary setback doesn't mean that you have to quit or give up on your goals. It means that you draw out the lessons, work on setting more short-term goals or more appropriate goals, and readjust goals as you come to know yourself and your present situation better. Your goal may simply be to do, or cope, the best you can on that day.

When I was younger, I used goal setting in a haphazard way. Now that I am more knowledgeable in this area, I am better able to set very specific goals and to adjust unmet goals by bringing them into line with myself, rather than trying to force myself into line with them. When there is a discrepancy, the goals are usually off target. *I am being who I am.* I am doing the best that I can at this moment, given the complexities of life. Goal setting doesn't provide all the answers, but when used properly it certainly does nudge you in the direction you want to go. Regardless of what you want to accomplish, setting goals and being positive with yourself are important. To think more positively or focus more completely, set some short-term goals to work on today, tomorrow, and every day. Put your goals up on the wall as a reminder. Give it a try. You've got nothing to lose and a lot to gain in terms of living closer to your potential.

CHAPTER 6

POSITIVE PERSPECTIVES

The key to living closer to your potential both in your performance domain and outside of it lies in developing your ability to carry a positive perspective and to view things in a constructive way.

Whenever an important performance or event is about to occur in your life, thoughts run through your head about probable consequences of the event. You say certain things to yourself or believe certain things about what might happen and how that will make you feel. These thoughts make you worry or free you from worry, make you feel confident or shatter your confidence.

What triggers your emotional reaction to an event is the way you perceive the event, or what you say to yourself about yourself in relation to it, rather than the event itself. A simple change in your perspective

THE ONE THING OVER WHICH YOU HAVE ABSOLUTE CONTROL IS YOUR OWN THOUGHTS. IT IS *THIS* THAT PUTS YOU IN A POSITION TO CONTROL YOUR OWN DESTINY.

PAUL G. THOMAS

about the meaning of a particular event, or in your belief about your capacity to cope with it positively, can change your current emotional reality. Nothing changes except the way you perceive yourself or interpret the event, and yet that simple positive change can give you inner strength and confidence, release you from stress, and free you to live or perform more joyfully.

Let's take performance anxiety as an example. If you listen to sportscasters (or "anxietycasters") and actually start to believe what they say, you might begin to believe that anxiety is external and inescapable, like rain pouring down from a dark cloud: "You can almost hear the tension out there . . . this is it . . . do or die . . . the world is watching . . . there's *real* pressure on these athletes here today." Yet some performers are able to enter these situations and stay focused without becoming overly anxious. They perform well and even feed off these challenging situations to improve their performance. How is that possible?

It is possible for the simple reason that anxiety doesn't float around out there waiting to pounce on you like some kind of bogeyman. It is strictly internal; in fact, anxiety does not exist outside your head. Certain situations may tend to get the adrenaline flowing, but you are not *required* to become anxious in these situations, and even if you do you can still perform well. Situations are not anxious, people are. You are anxious when you accept the situation as one that creates anxiety, or when you become overly concerned with outcomes or consequences. Performers who can enter the arena feeling excited but in control have repainted the anxiety-filled picture that others have often painted for them.

Don't wait until anxiety arises to seek strategies for coping with it. Prepare yourself to prevent unproductive anxiety from arising in the first place. Various techniques for on-site anxiety control, including shifts in focus and relaxation, can be effective in performance situations, but sometimes they don't get to the root of the issue, which is your acceptance of a situation as stressful. Your first line of anxiety prevention and control lies in your way of viewing yourself and the world around you. Above all, you must keep your own worth in perspective and know that it remains intact regardless of whether you meet a particular goal.

We experience stress and frustration in performance situations, as well as in other aspects of life, largely because we want to be perfect at everything we do. We want others to be perfect and we expect the situations we enter to be perfect, which of course they never are.

Sometimes we unknowingly set ourselves up for frustration because we have impossible expectations. Albert Ellis referred to the following perspectives or beliefs as interfering with our capacity to perform to our potential and live our lives joyfully (Ellis 1976, 25):

1. The belief that you must *always* have love and approval from all the people you find significant
2. The belief that you must *always* prove to be thoroughly competent, adequate, and achieving
3. The belief that emotional misery comes from external pressures and that you have little ability to control or change your own feelings
4. The belief that if something seems fearsome or threatening, you must preoccupy yourself with it and make yourself anxious about it
5. The belief that your past remains all-important and that because something once strongly influenced your life, it has to keep determining your feelings and behavior today

You cannot have the love and approval of all people at all times, no matter how much you give of yourself; nor can you always be thoroughly competent at all things. None of us is, or ever will be, perfect at all things at all times. We all screw up sometimes, and that's OK. That's being human.

The excessive worry that destroys skilled performance usually comes from exaggerating the importance of an event's outcome, from viewing it as if your physical or emotional life is at stake or as if your entire meaning on earth rests in the balance. We know this is not really the case, but we sometimes act as if it were. On rare occasions, in some high-risk events, a physical life may hang in the balance. But never is our emotional life or overall meaning really on the line in other performances, no matter how much we may tell ourselves, or how much others may lead us to believe, that it is.

If you approach a performance as if it is the only important event in the world, as if your life will be completely useless unless you do well, then you set yourself up for needless anxiety. If you incessantly worry about your performance or about appearing incompetent, you are probably too focused on negative possibilities or too concerned with what others might think. The worry is almost always worse than the event itself. Your performance (and people's reaction to it) rarely turns out to be as terrible as you might have imagined. But it would turn out a lot better if you did not dwell on the negative in the first place. You can lessen your worries and improve your performance by shifting your focus, and by viewing yourself, the event, and your performance in a more positive light.

The best performers approach events physically ready and mentally focused: *I've got a job to do; I'm capable of doing it, and I'll do it the best I can. Beyond that, I'm not going to worry about it.* If they do have a disappointing performance, they draw out the positive lessons and move on. They have learned to refocus effectively and to keep things in perspective. Think about your own situation: At one time you were no good in your performance domain at all—in fact, you hadn't even begun to participate in it. Yet you were an acceptable person and loved by those closest to you. Now that you are so much more skilled, why is it so disastrous to achieve a little less than perfection? You are still a skilled performer, a worthy human being, and you will continue to be acceptable and worthy long after you stop performing in this domain.

In every setback is an opportunity for personal growth.

I can no longer do a quadruple twisting back somersault on a trampoline; it's been over 10 years since I've done a triple; I can still do a double. Does that mean that I am half as good, half as worthy a person as I used to be? Does it mean that I'm twice as good a person as someone who cannot do even a single somersault? It would be ridiculous to think that my overall value as a person depends on my performance on any given night, but we sometimes do confuse the outcome of a performance with our human worth. When this happens, a more balanced perspective is needed: Our human essence extends far beyond our performance in a given task at a given time.

SHIFTING FOCUS TO BUILD CONFIDENCE AND REDUCE ANXIETY

The best way to permanently reduce unwanted and unproductive anxiety is to set realistic personal performance goals, to focus fully on executing your task, and to know in your heart that you remain a valued person regardless of the performance outcome. If you can approach potentially anxiety-provoking situations with a healthy perspective, then most debilitating anxiety will not surface. You will become positively energized, because you are excited and you need a certain level of intensity to perform well in your event. But you will not become anxious to a degree that will jeopardize your performance focus or your well-being afterward.

How do you go about changing perspectives? You begin by questioning some of your own thoughts—the ones that upset you in the first place. The next time you feel anxious, stop and ask yourself: *Why am I anxious? What am I thinking or saying to myself about the event, about myself, or my performance, or people's reaction, that is making me anxious? Do I have to see it this way or think or feel this way? Do I have to upset myself over this? Is it really worth continuing to worry about this? Is it doing me or anyone else any good?*

Set a personal goal to think less in ways that are likely to worry you and more in ways that will uplift you and others. Look for the legitimate support within yourself and your environment that gives you reason to believe in your capacity to meet the challenges you face successfully. Remind yourself of your strengths and of positive events in your past. You are fully capable of achieving your goals and changing your perspective if you constantly remind yourself to think and act in more positive ways.

Mentally preparing yourself to be more positive helps with this positive change process. Think about how you would prefer to respond in various situations in the future. Imagine yourself responding more effectively to situations that may have upset you unnecessarily in the past. Imagine yourself in the situation, thinking, focusing, believing, and acting in more constructive ways. Then work on replicating this more positive vision of yourself (or others) in the real world. With persistence, you'll win this one.

Sometimes just a conscious attempt to see things from a different perspective, or as they could be, leads to a change in the way you view a situation or yourself. As soon as you begin to tell yourself (and believe)—*Hey, that doesn't really matter; there's no reason to get upset about this; this doesn't mean I'm inadequate or not appreciated; I have the strength and balance to deal with this*—changes in your feelings are apparent. As soon as you begin to recognize and believe in your own worth and abilities—*Hey, I can do this; I can direct my own thoughts and focus; I can control my actions and reactions*—there's nearly always an immediate change in your own feelings and behavior.

Whenever you are able to influence a positive change in your focus or perspective, think about what you did or said to yourself to bring it about. Hang on to this for future use. Also, try to be aware of self-imposed obstacles to positive change, such as things you say to yourself that block your own progress: *This will never work; I can't do this; I'm no good; I'll probably mess it up;* and the like. What are you saying to yourself right now about your capacity to change the things you want to change? That's a good place to start establishing a positive perspective.

Sometimes reinterpreting your physical sensations is enough to put you back in control. Let's say that you get a knot in your stomach or your heart starts to thump hard just before a performance begins. You could say to yourself, *Oh man, I'm so nervous . . . I don't know what I'm going to do. . . . I'll probably blow it.* Or you could interpret these physical signals in a totally positive manner, and say, *The feeling in my stomach is the result of the secretion of adrenaline, which acts as a stimulant; what is actually happening is that my body is telling me I'm ready, let's go.*

Virtually every performer you have ever seen or competed against, including all the best athletes in the world, experience this rush of excitement before an important event. It shows that you care and want to do well. You can make it work for you by recognizing its positive elements and by channeling your focus into your performance.

A certain amount of intensity is necessary for good performances in mind-body endeavors. You wouldn't do too well if you were half asleep. You are looking for that optimal amount of "upness" where you feel just right. If you find yourself feeling too pumped up, you can make this work for you by using it as a signal to try to bring yourself down a bit, perhaps through shifting focus, relaxed breathing, or refocusing on the connection with your performance.

It is important to remember that no matter how you viewed things in the past, you are not obligated to keep viewing them in the same light. You may have thought of yourself as being necessarily anxious or reactive in certain situations in the past, but you can control and change how you feel about the situation, as well as how you react in the situation. By developing a positive plan of action and working to maintain a positive perspective, you can enter more situations in control, even situations that previously caused anxiety or performance problems.

Suppose that at the performance site, your thoughts start to drift to such things as how nervous you are or how terrible it would be if you blew it. What can you do about it? Use these thoughts as a reminder to shift your focus to something more constructive. Remember that you are capable of executing this performance; recall your simple goal of just doing the best you can do today; focus on your own preparation, your own warm-up, and doing your job—all of which are within your own control. Remind yourself of your best-performance focus, your good recent practices, and your ability to perform well. Remember that your overall value as a person remains. Self-assuring thoughts about your worth, your preparation, your readiness, your commitment, your capacity, and your best focus can help immensely, and they are based on facts—solid, positive facts.

Many important elements of your life, such as your performance and your perspective, are potentially within your control. Once you realize that you can effect positive change in these areas, you will, precisely because they are within your control. However, other important things in life are beyond your potential control. It is self-defeating to take responsibility or feel guilty for things that happen to you, or to others close to you, over which you have no direct influence. You cannot control things that are impossible to control, no matter how hard you try or how much responsibility you assume for doing so. You cannot control the past; you cannot control things that occur strictly by chance; you cannot control the actions, reactions, or incompetencies of all the people around you.

You and your goals are best served when you focus on things within your potential control. Your thoughts are within your control. Your thoughts direct your focus, confidence, and performance. Think about failure, and you become anxious. Think about errors, and they are yours. Think about your strengths, and you feel strong. Think that you *can*, and you will.

These positive self-suggestions can help you in your balanced pursuit of personal excellence:

- I am in control of my own thinking, my own focus, my own life.
- I am a good, valued person in my own right.
- I control my own thoughts and emotions, and direct the whole pattern of my performance, health, and life.
- I am fully capable of achieving the goals that I set for myself today. They are within my control.
- I control the step in front of me.
- I learn from setbacks, and through them I see room for improvement and opportunities for personal growth.
- I embrace the lessons from my experiences.
- My powerful mind and body are one. I free them to excel.
- Every day in some way I am better, wiser, more adaptable, more focused, more confident, more in control.
- I choose to live my life fully.
- I choose to excel.

PART III

MENTAL PREPARATION FOR EXCELLENCE

CHAPTER 7

MISSION TO EXCELLENCE

The pursuit of excellence begins with getting to know your own patterns. This is simply a process of becoming more aware of your own capabilities, strengths, and weaknesses. It also means becoming more aware of what you really want, as opposed to what others want of you. With this awareness, you can better establish priorities and thereby pursue the things that are really important to you and avoid the things that are not.

You know yourself better than anyone else in this world. You are already inside yourself. You just have to begin tuning in to how you usually think, feel, and react when you perform your best; how you interact with different types of people and events in your life when you are at your best; and how you cope with different kinds of

CHANGE AND GROWTH TAKE PLACE WHEN A PERSON HAS RISKED HIMSELF AND DARES TO BECOME INVOLVED WITH EXPERIMENTING WITH HIS OWN LIFE.

HERBERT OTTO

demands when you cope best. Performance settings provide beautiful opportunities for knowing yourself. You can listen to your body and feelings. You can discover what works for you and what works against you. You can find your best focus for rising to various challenges. How do you think, focus, and act when your situation improves? How is that different when your situation degenerates? How do you turn things around from negative to positive, bad to good, good to great? Take time to know yourself. It will serve you well, now and in the future.

Getting to know your own patterns also involves becoming aware of the direction of your own errors or imperfections. Do you usually err by overreacting or underreacting, by giving too little or giving too much? Do you usually work too hard or not hard enough? Do you begin too early or too late? Do you usually fall short when fresh or fatigued, active or passive? Do you miss to the left or right of the target, high or low? Do you overthrow or underthrow? Are you too emotional or not emotional enough, too relaxed or not relaxed enough, too serious or not serious enough? What are the patterns related to your best performances and your performance imperfections? Finding out what they are is a first step toward consistent improvement.

Focus Control and Commitment

The following two self-assessment scales are based on qualities that leading performers and coaches around the world use to describe the kind of commitment and focus that separates great performers from the rest, in a variety of performance domains. A rating of 10 means that the statement is completely true for you, a rating of 1 means that it is completely false, and a rating of 5 means that it is sometimes true and sometimes false.

Performers who excel rate themselves higher on both commitment and focus control than less-accomplished performers. They tend to have total scores in the high 80s or 90s on both the commitment scale and the focus control scale, or average scores of 9 or above for most individual items on both scales. The higher your commitment and the better your focus, the more likely you are to achieve your highest level of excellence.

Focus Control Rating Scale

Rate yourself on each item. Then go back and identify your strengths and the areas in which you can improve.

1. I get so absorbed in my performances (or experiences) that everything else disappears.

1	**2**	**3**	**4**	**5**	**6**	**7**	**8**	**9**	**10**
never									always

2. I can direct or redirect my focus so that it does me the greatest good, even if I become nervous or uptight in performance situations.

1	**2**	**3**	**4**	**5**	**6**	**7**	**8**	**9**	**10**
never									always

3. I maintain or quickly regain a high-quality focus in practice or preparation sessions.

1	**2**	**3**	**4**	**5**	**6**	**7**	**8**	**9**	**10**
never									always

4. I maintain or quickly regain a high-quality focus in performances or competitions.

1	**2**	**3**	**4**	**5**	**6**	**7**	**8**	**9**	**10**
never									always

5. I have a strong inner confidence, a feeling that I can do anything I set my mind to.

1	**2**	**3**	**4**	**5**	**6**	**7**	**8**	**9**	**10**
never									always

(continued)

6. I learn from criticism and take it as an opportunity to improve.

1	**2**	**3**	**4**	**5**	**6**	**7**	**8**	**9**	**10**
never									always

7. I handle bad calls or situations that go against me by getting right back on a positive path.

1	**2**	**3**	**4**	**5**	**6**	**7**	**8**	**9**	**10**
never									always

8. I stay motivated and focused even when behind or down in points.

1	**2**	**3**	**4**	**5**	**6**	**7**	**8**	**9**	**10**
never									always

9. I maintain my performance focus totally in the present, in the here and now (for example, one shot, one step, one moment at a time).

1	**2**	**3**	**4**	**5**	**6**	**7**	**8**	**9**	**10**
never									always

10. I quickly regain my best-performance focus even after an error or setback.

1	**2**	**3**	**4**	**5**	**6**	**7**	**8**	**9**	**10**
never									always

Total focus control score _____

Commitment Rating Scale

Rate yourself on each item. Then go back and identify your strengths, as well as those items that may require reassessment or realignment if excellence is to become a realistic goal.

1. I am willing to put aside other things to excel in my sport or chosen performance domain.

1	2	3	4	5	6	7	8	9	10
never									always

2. I really want to become an excellent performer in my sport or performance domain (or other chosen endeavor).

1	2	3	4	5	6	7	8	9	10
never									always

3. I prepare myself mentally for each practice and each performance so I can continue to get the best out of myself.

1	2	3	4	5	6	7	8	9	10
never									always

4. I am determined to never let up or give up (for example, I remain committed to achieve my goals, make the move, or complete the mission), even in the face of obstacles.

1	2	3	4	5	6	7	8	9	10
never									always

5. I take personal responsibility for mistakes and work hard to correct them.

1	2	3	4	5	6	7	8	9	10
never									always

(continued)

6. I give 100 percent focus and effort in practices or preparation sessions, whether it's going well or not.

1	**2**	**3**	**4**	**5**	**6**	**7**	**8**	**9**	**10**
never									always

7. I give 100 percent focus and effort in performances or competitions, whether it's going well or not.

1	**2**	**3**	**4**	**5**	**6**	**7**	**8**	**9**	**10**
never									always

8. I give everything I can, even when the challenge seems insurmountable or beyond reach.

1	**2**	**3**	**4**	**5**	**6**	**7**	**8**	**9**	**10**
never									always

9. I feel more committed to improvement in my performance domain (or other chosen endeavor) than to anything else.

1	**2**	**3**	**4**	**5**	**6**	**7**	**8**	**9**	**10**
never									always

10. I find great joy and personal fulfilment in my performance domain (or other chosen endeavor).

1	**2**	**3**	**4**	**5**	**6**	**7**	**8**	**9**	**10**
never									always

Total commitment score _____

What can you do to improve your focus or commitment? To improve your focus control, begin by drawing on your own experiences and the various strategies presented in this book. Develop a focusing plan to improve the quality or duration of your focus, and practice focusing fully every day.

Also, review your level of commitment. Given your current performance level, is your commitment strong enough to take you where you want to go? If not, take it up a notch. You can choose to raise your level of commitment to bring it into line with your goals, if you really want to achieve those goals. The other option is to adjust or lower your performance goals so that they are more realistic in terms of your current level of commitment; otherwise, you may experience continued frustration.

MISSION TO EXCELLENCE— STEPS TO FOLLOW

When I coach athletes and others on performance enhancement, I often pose a series of performance-related questions to which they respond. Together we discuss various options for self-growth, some of which they implement. Over the course of my life I have discovered that, with some basic guidelines to follow, most self-directed students and performers are fully capable of asking themselves these same questions and can successfully implement their own performance-enhancement strategies.

Following are six procedural steps designed to help you explore and act on your options for personal excellence:

1. Select a target area for improvement within your sport, performance domain, or life; or a situation in which you would like to have greater personal control; or an essential mental skill from the wheel of excellence that you would like to strengthen. Your specific target may be to improve your commitment, focus, confidence, positive imagery, mental readiness, distraction control, ongoing learning, or anything else that can increase the level and consistency of your performance or bring you closer to living your potential. Make sure you choose a meaningful target area on which to set your sights for positive change.

2. Complete the Mission to Excellence Interview (pages 87-89), keeping your target area in mind. This will help you pinpoint the

circumstances within your chosen target area that are related to your best performances or greatest control and to your less than best performances or least control. Reflect closely on what may have already worked well for you in some situations.

3. Review the strategies for excellence that are provided in this book. Choose some relevant options for improvement by drawing upon anything that you feel might be useful in accomplishing your mission to excellence. (If you want additional practical examples of how top athletes and other great performers have strengthened their mental game, along with their planning forms, consider also *Psyching for Sport, Embracing Your Potential, Psyched,* and the CD-ROM *Visions of Excellence.*) (See references and resources section, pages 235-236.)

4. Write down your plan of action for enhancing your performance or personal growth in the target area you selected. What are you going to do to initiate the change you are seeking? When are you going to it, how often, and in what circumstances?

5. Experiment with your plan by practicing it and applying the various strategies you selected in different situations in order to move closer to your goals. After implementing a strategy in practice or a performance situation, take a few minutes to think about what worked well, what didn't work, and what needs to be refined or changed to improve your plan and your performance. In order to continue to move closer to your goals, continue to assess and refine your plan by drawing out and acting on the lessons from your ongoing experiences.

6. Where feasible, get together with others pursuing excellence (for example, teammates, classmates, colleagues, friends, or family members). Share views on effective ways to pursue your goals, to enter and maintain the zone of full focus, or ways to become mentally stronger, more positive, more balanced, or more joyful in your pursuit.

This mission to excellence is a great opportunity for you to apply relevant mental skills training to something that you feel is important in your life. If you approach this six-step process with commitment to make a positive change, it will be an extremely valuable learning experience—and the chances of accomplishing your mission, or actually making the positive changes you are seeking, are very high. You can use this same process to bring about positive improvements in any part of your life.

Pursuing excellence requires you to focus on what you hope to achieve.

Thousands of students, athletes, and performers in a variety of domains have gained from this mission to excellence process, so I am confident that it can work for you. The first and final choice for self-growth and improving your situation always rests in your own hands. You decide.

Mission to Excellence Interview

The purpose of this interview is to clarify desired areas of improvement and target specific ways to make those improvements. Your mission to excellence project can focus on something you are doing that you would prefer not to do; or something you are not doing that you would prefer to do; or doing something better, more consistently, or more joyfully. The precise circumstances that surround your best and less than best experiences or performances in this specific situation should be thought out in detail, because this knowledge can help you make your desired improvements. It is very important to understand what you are already doing that allows you to perform well at some times, or in some situations. Keeping a performance notebook or personal diary that contains your reflections on how your attitude, focus, or thinking may have affected your performance positively or negatively is a good idea. It can help you understand more fully what works best for you.

It has become clear through my work with athletes and other performers that specific events within the environment and within a person's own thinking lead to consistent or inconsistent performance. Only at certain moments does effective focusing become a problem. For one Olympic figure skater, this happened only at important competitions, "when I see the judges peering over me as I begin and I start to think about being judged instead of focusing on the movement." For a world champion water skier, it was "when I approach the first buoy on my slalom run and I think, *Uh-oh, I'm probably going to blow this.*" For a national team basketball player, it was "when the coach yells at me during the game and I start to worry about him instead of concentrating on playing ball."

It is important to assess precisely when the problem arises and to become aware of what you are thinking, or what you are focused on, at that moment. It is also important to become aware of what you do or focus on when the situation, or your performance, improves. The following self-directed interview questions are designed to help you with this self-assessment and help you find your best focus for positive change. These interview questions have been used effectively as a guide to strengthen focus and enhance performance in sport, the performing arts, school, health, the workplace, relationships, and balanced living, so they should be relevant to your situation.

QUESTIONS

Here are some question you can ask yourself.

1. What is your target area for improvement?

2. What are you doing that you don't want to do, or failing to do that you would like to do? What would you like to change, make better, or act on more consistently?

3. Where, when, and under what circumstances is the greatest need or challenge for change or improvement? In what situations does a problem usually come up? What kinds of demands or expectations are being placed on you at that time? What are you thinking, feeling, or focusing on?

4. How important is it for you to improve your reaction or performance in this target area?

5. Think about the times when you have been in this situation and your focus, response, or performance has been at its best. What was going on then? What were you doing or saying to yourself? What were you focused on?

6. What about the times when your response or performance seemed at its worst? What was going on then? What were you doing or saying to yourself? Where was your focus?

7. What seems to be the major difference between your best and less than best responses, experiences, or performances with respect to

    a. taking care of your own needs for rest, nutrition, personal space, and simple joys?

    b. what you are thinking about before the experience or performance (for example, your attitude, focus, or feeling going into it)?

    c. what you are focused on during the experience or performance?

    d. what is going on around you, or what others around you are doing or not doing?

8. What do you think you can do to improve the situation, your response to it, or your performance within this situation?

9. Have you made a strong enough commitment to make a change in this target area by regularly *practicing* or working at improving your focus, response, or performance in this area? Are you prepared to make that commitment now?

SELECTING A STRATEGY
FOR IMPROVEMENT

Once you have completed your interview, you are faced with the delightful task of selecting effective strategies for making the changes you are seeking. "How do I choose the best one?" you're asking, right?

Throughout this book I present those strategies for excellence that I use most often in my individual consultations with athletes and others pursuing personal excellence. For additional options and examples, see *Embracing Your Potential, Psyching for Sport, Psyched,* and the CD-rom *Visions of Excellence.*

Before choosing a strategy for your target area of improvement, read through various options, along with the examples that show how different performers have used them. Keep in mind where you want to end up. Some approaches will be immediately more attractive to you than others, or will simply seem more suitable for you in this situation. You may read about one strategy and think, *That will never work for me*... and you will probably be right. As you read about another strategy, you might find yourself thinking, *Hmm, maybe that one will work.* Try any strategy that makes intuitive sense to you. If it feels right just reading about it, try it.

Through my consultation with thousands of athletes and other performers, one thing has come through loud and clear—the uniqueness of individual mental preparation, motivation, and coping. An approach that may work beautifully for you may have the opposite effect on someone else. For example, in the same precompetition situation, one athlete may best prepare by thinking about something relaxing or joyful away from sport (to clear the mind), while another prefers to focus on the task at hand (to direct the mind), and a third accepts the tensions and channels that emotional energy in positive directions. Each approach works, but does so for unique individuals.

Your belief about the potential effectiveness of a particular strategy influences your commitment to work on it and, consequently, how well it will work for you. Usually your beliefs about what might be effective for you do not grow out of a vacuum; they are the result of many years of living with yourself. It would be difficult to have lived this long without knowing something about how you function. So your beliefs about what will or will not work for you often rest on a sound foundation. They are based on the number of years you have lived and the extent to which you have experimented with your own life. Try to read through the various options with an open mind. Then follow your feelings on strategy selection.

It is often best to select several approaches or strategies that seem appropriate for your particular situation. Then experiment with these strategies until you can isolate what works best for you. It may be a single approach, a combination of several interrelated approaches, or a personal strategy that you have come up with yourself. The fact that something has not yet worked does not mean that it cannot work. Sometimes you just have not committed to give it a chance. Often all that you need is more persistence in practicing and implementing the strategies that have already been somewhat successful in your past. If something works for you, then use it, because that's the bottom line.

CHAPTER 8

QUEST FOR CONSISTENCY

Those who consistently perform close to potential have learned to control their focus, channel their emotions, and bounce back from setbacks in a constructive way. They have refined the ability to shift quickly from negative thinking to a positive focus, particularly in response to self-doubts, anxiety, errors, or setbacks. If you don't learn to do this, your chances of getting the most out of your preparation sessions and the best out of yourself when it counts most will be dramatically reduced. The mental skills required to perform your best are developed long before the day of the contest through hours of quality preparation and through experiences that teach you to maintain or regain control over your own mental state.

CONTROL YOUR EMOTIONS, OR THEY WILL CONTROL YOU.

REACTING TO IMPERFECTIONS
OR ERRORS

Constructive reaction to errors or imperfections is a skill you can learn. Many people react to setbacks or loss by becoming upset with themselves, angry at others, or depressed. If they fall behind or face an obstacle, they lose focus, cease to perform well, or feel like giving up. The earlier you learn to react in a positive or constructive way, the better.

A setback within a game or performance (for example, making a mistake) can drag you down; it can also serve as a reminder to focus more fully on the next step, to redirect your energy in a more positive way, or to analyze errors at an appropriate time. After games or performances, the best performers mentally replay key moves and turning points, and always try to find lessons that will help them for the next outing. They carefully review what went well and what can be improved. They may be disappointed or frustrated, but they have learned to pass through it quickly by extracting and acting on constructive lessons that can help them in the future. As one of the world's best athletes expressed it, "As a less-experienced player I reacted more emotionally; I was angry at myself. Now I concentrate more in the game, analyze errors or losses at an appropriate time, replay key shots and turning points, and draw out important lessons."

One player experienced real problems with emotional outbursts during games. "If I lost a rally, I hated my opponent. . . . I would get so angry that I could lose eight points in a row because of that. I had problems controlling my temper to the point of shouting and breaking rackets." He made a strong effort to get his temper and focus under control. When he played with controlled focus, he played as well as anyone. One strategy he used when he got angry was to try to take advantage of his anger by constructively directing his burst of energy into the next rally, to "hustle more," "be totally ready," "move faster," and "smash harder." This shifted his focus away from anger (at himself or his opponent) and reconnected him to playing the game with a renewed vigor.

What's wrong with getting angry or upset? Most importantly, it interferes with your reason for being there, whether you are seeking enjoyment, consistency, or a high-quality performance. Its effects are probably most detrimental if you begin to condemn yourself or others during the program, event, or interaction, because you take your best focus away from the remaining tasks. If you are mentally chastising yourself because of the last shot, move, or event, you cannot at the same time be focusing on the present skill or preparing for your next move. You can't dwell on how you blew the last shift or routine and at the same time perform well in this moment. You have to clear your mind of negative thoughts about what has passed and worries about what might follow in order to free your body and mind to perform in the present.

Find a way to learn something positive from every experience.

Someone who flies off the handle or dwells on the negative might say, "Oh, but it doesn't matter that much if I do it during practices or my daily life." Ah, but it does. If you become practiced at negative thinking during daily training or living, there's a very good chance it will carry over into relationships and competitions. Moreover, it takes away the joy of sport and life. There are enough obstacles along the path to personal excellence; there is no advantage in adding negative thinking or self-putdowns. Staying positive, relaxed, and focused is particularly important for regaining the flow of a performance or relationship, particularly after an error, argument, or setback. It is essential for coming back successfully. If you do not learn to pass quickly from negative emotions to a constructive focus, then what you really want will slip away from you.

To speed up this learning process, think about how you would prefer to respond in these situations, set personal goals for improving your focus control, and work toward achieving those goals. The next time something goes wrong in a game, routine, or relationship, use that as a signal to focus on doing what you know will enhance the rest of your performance or interaction. For example, during a gymnastics routine, a skating program, or team game, let any thoughts about the error slip away by focusing fully on the next move or perhaps on a flash of finishing well. In a sport where there is a break from intense concentration, such as a racket sport, quickly analyze the reason for the error (for example, while walking back to receive the serve); take a deep, relaxing breath; and focus on what you want to do next.

You may have excellent physical and technical skills, but you will never perform consistently to your full capacity unless you gain control of your mental state. Channel your emotions, control your focus, and perform your best.

This was a lesson learned through experience by a top Swedish sportsman. As a rookie he quickly discovered that as soon as he got upset, he couldn't play well. As a result of this knowledge, he grew into a veteran with a different approach: "I practiced reacting the way I wanted to react, which changed my feeling going into the game. I could go in with more confidence. . . . I tried to think about what caused a mistake and correct it. I thought about what made me lose and analyzed it. I was disappointed, but I tried to learn from it." This athlete's early recognition of the critical importance of focus control, along with his commitment to continually improve, allowed him to become one of the best in the world.

CASE STUDIES IN SELF-CONTROL

Pat Messner, professional musician and former world champion in water skiing, reflected on how she went about gaining greater personal control in practice and in competition.

■ I first began competition when I was 10 years old. At that time, I felt that having days where nothing goes right and everything goes wrong, days where I felt I was the worst competitor on earth, and days when I would be mad at anything, was all part of the competitive life.

I was wrong, and it wasn't an easy thing to find out. It happened because of an experience I had in the Western Hemisphere Championship in Mexico. It was in March, and that was during our off-season. During the practice session, I couldn't do anything right. I felt like I had never skied as badly. This practice session made me believe that there was no way I was going to place . . . let alone win! I decided I might as well relax and enjoy myself.

Before the actual event, I went through my usual stretching and warm-up. The only difference was that I wasn't thinking about what was to come. I just sat down on the grass, listened to some music, and waited for my turn. This was very unusual for me, because I'm usually very nervous. I just didn't seem to care. I listened to the music and relaxed.

Believe it or not, I've never had a better tournament. I skied better than I ever had before. Not only that, but I became Western Hemisphere Champion.

What did all this prove? It proved to me that if I could stay relaxed and calm at all my tournaments, maybe I'd always ski better.

Since that time I have learned many things that may be as helpful to you as they were to me. I've tried a number of different methods of relaxation. The method I found best is a simple thing anyone can do anytime, anyplace. Sit down or lie down and listen to some relaxing music. I can take my portable cassette right down to the dock and listen to music till it's time for me to ski. I let my mind do what it likes. I don't take responsibility for my thoughts. I just let them pass by. If you don't like music, then try reading a book. I also found this to be very helpful.

Another important thing for me is mental practice. I run through my event mentally just as if it was real. I try to feel as if I am actually doing the run. If you find it hard to "feel" yourself or you can't picture yourself, watch a video of yourself or someone you admire. Sometimes it helps to give yourself audio cues as you go. I also try to simulate as many tournament conditions as possible in practice so that if unusual conditions should occur, I won't be as affected by them.

Sometimes it seems that the better you are, the easier it is to get upset by "little" things. I found that if I moved my attention away from what was making me angry and thought about something else, I'd feel better. Sometimes I set a goal for myself, like, the next two out of three times I get a chance to get mad, I won't. Most days it worked pretty well. On other days, the more I tried not to get mad or upset, the madder I got. It's days like that when I'm probably better off having a day of rest rather than practicing. Continuing to practice when I'm upset accomplishes absolutely nothing."

To try to improve her focus control during practices, Pat did a mission-to-excellence project following the procedures outlined in this book. Her goal was to make the best of as many practice sessions as possible in preparation for the world championships. Here are three self-control strategies she chose to implement:

• **Relax.** Try to physically relax yourself . . . calm yourself. Take deep breaths and feel your body get loose as you exhale. Pat and her coach tried a little experiment. "Each time I frowned he'd tell me, and I'd try to correct the situation. I found that when I did, my whole body felt more relaxed and I could do the trick easier."

• **Focus on correction.** Focus your attention on how to correct mistakes, instead of getting mad at yourself. If there are any errors, repeat the move mentally, correcting the errors, before trying it again. When practice is going well, write down what you think might be some of the reasons for it. Refer to this list to improve future situations.

• **Encourage yourself.** Avoid statements such as, *You dummy; you can't do anything right; you will never make it to the championships; give up.* Remind yourself of the facts. It's not that you can't do anything right, you're simply doing one little thing wrong. Praise yourself for all the things you are doing right.

Pat experimented with each of these strategies, sometimes stopping practice for five minutes to attempt to change her mood. As she said, "If you do not change the way you feel, the rest of the practice will be a waste of time." She found all of these strategies effective, but none of them perfect. They worked well most of the time; but she still got upset every now and then, no matter what she tried. Under these circumstances, Pat sometimes found it helpful for her coach to remind her of what she had accomplished, or to point out that she was being silly. "My behavior either got corrected, or he convinced me to take the day off." She found it most helpful to have a coach "who makes me realize that I'm only human."

If, after multiple attempts, a problem was not rectified, Pat could still leave practice knowing she had given it a good shot, but it was not working that day. Even though the problem is happening less and less, it still happens now and then. Everyone occasionally has a bad day or even a bad week. There's no sense in getting upset about it. Take the rest of the day off. Learn from it. Come in fresh tomorrow.

I can think of one gifted young athlete who could have gained from some of Pat's strategies for mood control. At age 11 she had Olympic potential. She could learn in a few attempts what others often take months to learn. But if she missed something or made an error, she cried, pouted, and stormed around for the rest of the day. According to her coach, "If she makes an error in one of her routines during practice or during a competition, it throws her whole concentration off. She then gives up and either refuses to finish the routine or, if she does finish, it is done very poorly. If practice is not going well for her, she will cry, and the rest of the practice is ruined."

This young woman had visions of becoming an Olympic champion, but instead retired after an unhappy two years because of an inability to get her moods under control. Perhaps if she had followed some of the strategies outlined here, her path would have unfolded in a different direction.

Sandy, a talented young female gymnast, had just made the team to compete in Europe. After that, she had two weeks of consistently bad workouts. She and the coach had been arguing regularly, and her coach had not spoken to her at all for the last couple of days. She had two weeks left before departing for her first international competition.

The coach called to ask if I could help. Sandy and I stretched ourselves out on a blue mat in the corner of the gym and had a nice talk. She confirmed the bad workouts and arguments, and expressed a sincere concern about being ready for her meet in Europe. She told me that workouts usually started out OK but that she became upset when the coach said something negative, such as "That's terrible"; "You don't listen"; or "You don't try." At that point the workout would begin to slide. This led to more negative comments or no interaction, bad feelings, and some tears—overall, a lousy workout.

"Sandy," I said, "we know the coach isn't perfect, but then not many of us are. She says some very negative things, and I've talked to her about giving more positive comments. She's improving, but it's a difficult thing for her to do. An important point for you to keep in mind is that this is her way of trying to help you. She does care, and she does want you to improve—to be ready for the meet—and you want that too. At this point I think it is easier for you to control your reaction to her than it is to rely on her to change. You can, in fact, control your own moods if you really want to."

Sandy said she really did want to improve the gloomy practice mood, and agreed to give the self-control approach a try. "What do you think about before a bad mood begins?" I asked.

"I think, *The coach hates me; she thinks I'm no good; she's mean to me; I'm never going to do this right.*"

"What do you feel when a bad mood begins? Are there physical sensations you are aware of? Are there certain emotions that begin to surface? Do you know when it's starting to happen?"

Sandy did have specific thoughts and personal signals of an impending mood change, though she had never thought about them before. She discussed some of them, and I gave her this advice: "OK. When you start to experience these thoughts or feelings—these personal signals—take a deep breath. Say to yourself, *Relax.* Then say to yourself, *Turn this thing around . . . you want to have a good workout . . . she's here to help . . . you are not going to waste the night feeling lousy . . . you can control this.* Then immediately focus on the trick you're trying to do or the routine you're trying to improve. Run it through your mind. Then go. *Do it.*

"Your challenge for the next week is to look for any signals of a bad mood coming on, then turn it around before it gets to the destructive stage. Don't let it ruin your workout, and don't let it drive you to tears. You may not be successful in turning around every bad mood right away, but if you can do it even half the time, that's a big improvement. That's success. Even doing it once is better than what is happening now. Your ultimate goal is to be able to turn potentially bad situations into good ones all the time. You have the capacity to do this, and you are the only one who can do it because you are the person who controls your own thoughts and your own focus."

We devised a little mood chart to help Sandy assess her feelings and record her progress through the next two weeks (see below). At the start of each practice she recorded her prepractice mood on the mood chart. For each event, she also recorded her mood at the start of the event, mood changes within the event, and her mood at the end of the event. If her mood had changed within the event, she indicated this by marking the face it had changed to. If it had changed more than once during the event, she drew an arrow from one face to the next, indicating the changes that took place. At the end of practice Sandy recorded her postpractice mood.

You can adapt this chart to suit your own needs whether it is in sport or other parts of your life. The comments section on the chart is primarily to help you discover what influences your mood. If your mood begins to decline and you are able to stop the slide or improve your disposition, then jot down what you did or said to yourself to turn things around. This will help you to discover what works best for you, as well as what does not work. You will then be in a better position to use things that work (for example, key words, images, or positive thoughts or actions) whenever you need them.

Let's take a look at what happened to Sandy's mood control the first week:

- **Day 1.** We discussed Sandy's concerns and the use of the mood chart approach.
- **Day 2.** She started practice feeling happy and ended feeling so-so. Her pattern the previous week had been to start feeling happy and end feeling sad.
- **Day 3.** She started practice feeling so-so and ended feeling very happy. She demonstrated to herself that she could lift her mood.
- **Day 4.** She started practice feeling sad, actually feeling sick. She was able to work through this and end feeling happy after a productive workout.
- **Day 5.** She started feeling happy and ended feeling very happy. She was starting to get things under control.

At the week's end Sandy and I went over her mood charts. Both of us were pleased with her progress. I asked her to think about a few things:

- What are your main thoughts or signs of a bad mood about to come on?

- What has worked best for preventing or overcoming bad moods?

- What hasn't worked at all?

- Where can you focus for further improvement in mood control during the coming week?

Sandy's mood charts showed further improvement the following week, and she left for Europe feeling excited and more in control. As her self-awareness and her strategies for mood control continued to improve, the necessity for conscious attempts to control and chart her moods declined. She learned to maintain control more of the time and to solve many problems before they arose. If her mood did occasionally start to slide, she knew from experience that she could control it (almost all of the time).

Karin, a teenage gymnast, was very inconsistent in both practice and meets. One day she could do everything well, and the next day she could blow everything. Karin told me that she knew whether it would be a good day or bad day before she got into the gym. If she had had a long day or felt at all sluggish, she would take those thoughts and that mood into the workout with her.

"Karin," I began, "unless you are seriously overtrained or ill, no matter how you feel on the way into the gym, you can turn things around to have a productive workout. Haven't you ever felt sluggish before practice and still had a good workout?" She had. "How is that possible? It is possible because you have the same body and the same skills that you had yesterday, when you had a good day. On your sluggish day, if your life depended on it, you could not only mount the beam, but you could jump over it and still have enough reserve energy to throw it across the gym.

"The next time you 'know you're going to have a bad day,' surprise yourself. Leave your negative thoughts in your locker. When you step through the gym door, decide that you are going to have a great day. When you see that apparatus, challenge yourself to feel strong, feel energetic, feel radiant. Remind yourself why you are here. If you are here, you might as well make the best of it. Why waste two or three hours? Focus fully for at least one event so you leave having had a good workout on something. If you can do it once, even in one event, you know you can do it again. When you do energize yourself on a sluggish day, or turn a negative feeling into a positive, try to be aware of how you have done it so you can do it again and again. You may not always have a super workout, but most days can be good days, and you can make those not-so-good days better than they might otherwise have been."

Karin's pattern of being "up today, down tomorrow" was not restricted to training sessions. In her last competition she fell on every routine, even though she had done these same routines in practice. Why? In her own words, "I knew I would have a bad day because I had a bad warm-up."

Does a warm-up that feels good or bad really have anything to do with your capacity to perform your routines in competition? Isn't a physical warm-up primarily to prepare your body for action, through stretching and movement? Haven't you ever seen someone have a lousy warm-up (for example, miss some tricks) and a great competition? It happens lots of times, and it can happen to you.

Your capabilities extend far beyond your warm-up. If you need a little proof, wait for a day when you come in feeling less than great in warm-up, and challenge yourself to a good performance. If you can do that once, in practice, you can go into the competition knowing and believing that even after a bad warm-up, things don't have to fall apart. You can still do your routines well as long as you focus fully on executing these moves. Figure skater Katarina Witt missed some important moves in her on-ice warm-up at the Olympic Games. She still nailed them in her routine and won the gold medal.

In the same way that your warm-up is separate from your performance, the first event or first shift is separate from the second and the second from the third. A poor showing in one event, skill, or shift in no way means you must have a poor showing in the next. The negative thoughts that you have after blowing one thing are what set you up for blowing the next. If you are convinced that because you blew the last one, you will probably blow this one, then you probably will. Your body will shrug its shoulders and say, "Who am I to argue with the thoughts and messages you are transmitting to me? If you, who are the master, say I'm going to blow it—I guess I'll follow orders and blow it."

On the other hand, if you know, as I know, that the next event, move, or shift really has nothing to do with the last one—that if you focus fully you are fully capable of performing at least as well as you ever have, regardless of what you did the last time—then you free your body to explore its present potential.

If you think about your real capabilities, about why you can do this, perhaps something will click and you will say to yourself, "Hey, that's right—why should that affect this . . . it doesn't really have to. If I focus on what I am doing, I can really do this." That may seem like a small step, but its impact can be gigantic. You may catch yourself thinking negatively from time to time (for example, *I messed that up, so I'll probably mess this up too*). But if you have already thought about how unproductive that kind of thinking is and have planned something constructive to focus on, you can often turn things around right on the spot. For example, you might say to yourself, *Stop . . . I can do as well here as I've ever done . . . now get focused and do it.*

Let your thoughts encourage you and remind you of what you can do; then focus fully on doing it.

MOOD CONTROL

NEARLY ALL DIFFICULTIES ARE OF OUR OWN MAKING AND ARE THE RESULT OF WRONG OR CONFUSED THINKING.

NELLIE MELBA, LEGENDARY OPERA SINGER, 1903

It's *your* mood! You can turn it around by thinking positive, happy, or focused thoughts, almost anytime or anywhere—in the morning, on the way to practice, in relationships, or stepping onto the competitive floor.

I can remember waking up one dull rainy morning, looking out the window, and thinking, *Yuck, what a miserable day.* But instead, I rolled over and thought, *Go out and enjoy the rain. Find the beauty and joy of today in as many ways as possible.* I turned that gloomy day around with that one thought and ended up laughing and smiling and enjoying the rain. What would otherwise have been a gray, drab day became one of beautiful gentleness and joy.

When you step out into the morning air, look for the good within the day and within yourself. Most mornings are beautiful, and there is beauty in every day—the sky, the dawn, the trees, the flowers, the sun, even the rain. Find the positive—*It's a great day for a run. It's a super day for a game; It's a great day to be alive.*

Mood control also means not upsetting yourself needlessly over things that don't really matter, unfamiliar circumstances, or events you cannot control. When our athletes compete in countries that are culturally different from our own, it is clear that the best performers are those who do not allow the food, the accommodations, or the system to negatively affect their performance. They view these things as relatively unimportant (which they are) and rely on the thoroughness of their overall mental and physical preparation. As one lad put it, "I'm one tough, finely tuned athlete." He proceeded to upset one of the top-seeded Russian wrestlers in Moscow.

Thinking the right way before you get out of bed in the morning, particularly on an important day, can start you out on the right track. Try focusing on thoughts like these: *Today is going to be a great day. I'm going to accomplish what I set out to do. I feel strong. I'm loaded with energy. I'm ready and I am going to do it. I am going to really live this day.*

Positive, action-oriented thoughts can help put you in the right frame of mind, no matter how you are feeling when you first open your eyes to the daylight. Do something that makes you feel the way you want to feel—connected, capable, and productive.

Mood control is a positive element of mind control, and it is within your grasp. It is largely a matter of looking for the good—in yourself, in your situation, in the world—and seeking out the gentleness in the storm.

TAKING CONTROL TO AVOID NEGATIVE MOODS

If you have a tendency to be negative, it is important that you learn to control your negative emotions—or they will ultimately have a negative effect on you, your performance, and your relationships. Uncontrolled negative emotions have the capacity to fuel the flames of your own destruction. The sooner you learn to shift away from negative thoughts to something more positive, the sooner you will take control of your performance and your life. Top performers experience setbacks, fatigue, fear, stress, and self-doubts, just like everyone else. However, they have developed the skills for letting their negative thoughts go and refocusing on the positives. As soon as you start to focus on doing the little things that free you to feel your best and be your best, you put yourself back in control of your mood and your performance.

You are one simple shift in focus away from regaining a positive perspective. One simple positive thought or positive action can do it. Make that shift sooner rather than later, and you will save yourself, and others, a lot of unnecessary anguish. At some point you will make that positive shift in focus anyway, so why not plan to make it now?

Positive perspectives are vital because they inspire us, energize us, and bring meaning and joy to our pursuits. They generate positive emotions that free us to do the good things we want to do, alone and together. Negative perspectives do the opposite. They drain energy that could otherwise be channeled in positive directions. So there is no value in dwelling on the negatives. If you can change the thought, perspective, or interpretation that led you to the negative emotions, you can almost always move to a more positive reality. You gain control over negative emotions by taking control of your thoughts. You do have a choice here. Positive thoughts and positive change begin with you.

If you find yourself slipping into a negative frame of mind and you would prefer to remain more positive, consider the following steps:

PREPARE YOURSELF TO BE MORE POSITIVE

Try the following suggestions to improve your perspective.

• Get more rest. It is easier to slip into negative thinking when you are tired or fatigued, so find a way to get enough rest, either for short times during the day or at night.

• Find ways to reduce the stress in your life. When there is more stress in your life, you are more susceptible to negative shifts in mood.

• Do one thing each day that is just for you—something you really enjoy. This can lift your spirits.

• Keep track of the good things that happen to you each day. Write down the simple, joyful things that lift you each day—in and out of your performance domain. The more positives you can find and appreciate, the less likely you are to be overcome by negatives.

• Open yourself to really experience your own successes and your own positive emotions when they do occur. Soak in them for a while. Remember them. Revisit them.

• Remain open to the positive emotions of the people around you. They can provide you with positive energy, inspiration, and perspective.

PROTECT YOURSELF FROM THE NEGATIVES

If you're having negative thoughts try some of the following tactics.

• Commit yourself to stop dwelling on the negatives. Plan to shift your focus to start dwelling on the positives.

• Commit to stop revisiting things that went wrong in the past, whether in a performance or a relationship. Start shifting your focus to revisit what went right.

• If you find your mind slipping back to the same negative memories (or experiences) again and again, tell yourself to stop! Then change channels to something more uplifting.

• If you look for the negatives in positives, start looking for the positives in negatives.

• If a negative thought or image pops into your mind, let it go, release it, erase it, let it float away. Don't let it consume you.

• If you can't just let the negative thought go, then shift your focus to something positive—a positive memory or uplifting experience that reflects a more positive reality (for example, think of something that clearly demonstrates that you have the capacity to perform well, or that confirms that you are in fact special and loved, or think of something fun to do and then do it).

• If the negative thought returns, shift back to a positive memory, a positive vision of the future, or a positive action in the present. Keep going back to positives every time that negative thought creeps into your mind. If you are persistent in doing this, you will eventually win over that negative thought.

PLAN FOR POSITIVE ACTION

Remember, you can accomplish almost anything with a good plan.

• There are two options for positive change—change your mind or change your environment. If you change your environment and maintain the same frame of mind, nothing will change. If you change your mind-set, everything will change.

- Develop a personal plan for remaining positive more often and for getting back on track more quickly, with as little self-inflicted pain as possible.

- Set a time limit for remaining negative or moping around. Then move on. Plan a positive path.

- Act on your plan.

- If you are not feeling the way you want to feel, step back and take a break. Do something you really like to do. Find your own space. Clear your mind. Clear your path.

- Pause long enough to breathe and relax. Let your mind and body relax. Drift to positive thoughts, positive images, and positive parts of your experiences, performances, and future.

- Practice staying positive and shifting focus from negative to positive whenever the opportunity arises.

- Follow your own best path.

CHAPTER 9

POSITIVE IMAGES

I'm sure images have run through your mind at some time or other. Take a moment to think of yourself doing your favorite activity, seeing a person you love, eating your favorite food, or relaxing in a quiet place. Go ahead—close your eyes and do this now.

Did an image or feeling flash through your mind as you thought of any of these? Perhaps you have not made use of your images in a highly refined or systematic way, but you have experienced it.

Before making an important phone call, did you ever mentally rehearse what you wanted to say? In the same way, through mental imagery you can prepare yourself to respond more effectively to expected—and unexpected—things that might happen.

YOUR IMAGES LEAD YOUR REALITY. THEY ALWAYS HAVE AND ALWAYS WILL.

Mental imagery gives you a chance to deal effectively with a problem or event in your head before you confront it in real life. If a challenge does arise, you are better able to handle it or cope with it. This is largely because you have already faced the challenge, have practiced some means of coping with it, and have overcome it in your mental reality, if not your physical reality. By using mental imagery, you can enter a variety of real situations, including competitions, with feelings like *I've been here before. It's no big surprise. There's no reason to panic. I've prepared for this; I can handle it.*

I've used this approach in preparing to deal more effectively with unexpected requests for talks or workshops. There are a limited number of hours in a day and in a life. If I want to achieve certain goals, I must have priorities. So if I receive a request to do something that means taking time from my family or another treasured activity, I listen to the request politely, note the information, and say that I will check my schedule. After I'm off the phone, when I am alone and not feeling pressured, I think about what the request entails in terms of my time, my priorities, and my various commitments. Do I really want to do this? Do I really have to do this? I often let such a decision work itself through while I'm running or walking in nature. Images of what the request entails often pop into my head. If at the end of my run I'm really excited about doing it, I agree; if not, I will most likely decline. Taking a bit of time to decide whether I want to do something puts me more in control of my life and, in this case, lets me prepare to communicate my decision firmly, politely, and without feeling guilty. When I do say no, I always try to recommend someone else who can do a good job, who might have fewer demands and enjoy fulfilling the request. Preparing yourself to do the things you want to do with the help of mental imagery is an effective way of freeing yourself to feel more comfortable, more relaxed, and more in control.

POSITIVE IMAGERY IN SPORT

In sport, mental imagery is used primarily to help you get the best out of yourself in training and in competition. Athletes who make the fastest progress and those who ultimately become their best make extensive use of performance imagery. They use it daily as a means of directing what will happen in training, and as a way of pre-experiencing their best competition performances. Mental imagery often starts out simply as you think through your goals, your moves, and your desired competitive performances. With practice, you will eventually be able to draw on various senses to experience in your mind the flawless execution of many of your goals, moves, performances, and coping strategies.

For many years, an Olympic figure skater had experienced inconsistency with a particular skill. I asked her to try to visualize herself doing it while I was sitting with her. She was unable to imagine herself completing the skill successfully. Either she would see herself making an error (the same one she usually made in the real world) and stop at that point, or the image would break up. I asked her to mentally practice doing that skill for approximately 10 minutes every night for a week. We took it in steps: first, she tried to get past the point where she made the error or the image broke up, without worrying about her form.

It took several nights of mental practice for her just to get through that point in imagery. Once she did, she began working on consistently getting through the complete skill in imagery. Finally, she focused on feeling herself do the skill as perfectly and fluidly as possible several times in a row. As soon as she began to feel herself skating the skill flawlessly in imagery, she also started to do it correctly in real practice situations. Within two weeks of our initial session, she was doing that skill with more quality and more consistently than she had ever done it.

This skater usually did her mental imagery in the evening just before going to sleep. She would lie in bed, close her eyes, and try to call up the desired feeling as clearly as possible. Later she began to run through the figure in imagery just before actually doing it on the ice. Finally, while standing in the arena at a competition, she was able to look at the ice, map out her program, and feel herself going through it flawlessly; this set the stage for a good performance.

Many athletes find it helpful to imagine and feel themselves performing skills perfectly immediately before competitive performances. High jumpers feel their ideal jumps, divers their perfect dives, skiers their best runs, gymnasts their perfect routines; archers follow their arrows to the center of the target. Team sport athletes run through key offensive moves, quick transitions, and great defensive moves. This process strengthens confidence by calling up the feeling of a best performance, and focuses full attention on the task at hand. It serves as a last-minute reminder of the focus and feeling you want to carry into the game or performance. It takes your mind away from thoughts of worry or self-doubt, gives a positive boost to your confidence, and frees your body to perform.

Mental imagery can also be valuable after a particularly successful performance, when the performance feeling is still fresh. It allows you to re-experience and hang on to successful aspects of the performance, which can help in preparing for your future best performances. Doing mental imaging is also highly effective when you have limited practice time, are making a comeback, or are recovering from an injury.

THE BEST IMAGES

The world's best athletes have extremely well-developed imagery skills. They use imagery daily to prepare themselves to get what they want out of training, to perfect skills within training sessions, to make technical corrections, to overcome obstacles, to imagine themselves succeeding in competition, and to strengthen their belief in their capacity to achieve their ultimate goals.

The refined performance imagery that highly successful athletes have developed involves feeling as if they are actually doing the skill and feeling the sensations. Even the best athletes, though, typically do not have good control over their mental imagery at first. They perfect this mental skill through persistent daily practice.

■ PICTURING THE PERFECT DIVE

I did my dives in my head all the time. At night, before going to sleep, I always did my dives. Ten dives. I started with a front dive, the first one that I had to do at the Olympics, and I did everything as if I was actually there. I saw myself in the pool at the Olympics doing my dives. If the dive was wrong, I went back and started over again. For me it was better than a workout. I felt like I was on the board. Sometimes I would take the weekend off and do imagery five times a day. It took me a long time to control my images and perfect my imagery, maybe a year, doing it every day. At first I couldn't see myself, I always saw everyone else, or I would see my dives wrong all the time. I would get an image of hurting myself, or tripping on the board, or I would "see" something done really bad. As I continued to work at it, I got to the point where I could feel myself on the board doing a perfect dive and hear the crowd yelling at the Olympics. I worked at it so much, it got to the point that I could do all my dives easily. Sometimes I would even be in the middle of a conversation with someone and I would think of one of my dives and "do it" (in my mind).

Sylvie Bernier, a former Olympic champion in springboard diving, shared how she developed incredible imagery skills in preparation for her flawless Olympic performance.

■ LISTENING TO YOUR FEELINGS

My imagery is more just feel. I don't think it is visual at all. I get this internal feeling. When I'm actually doing the skill on the ice, I get the same feeling inside. It is a very internal feeling that is hard to explain. You have to experience it, and once you do, then you know what you are going after. I can even get a feeling for an entire program. Sometimes in a practice I get myself psyched into a program that will win. I step on the ice and go to my starting position and I get this feeling, *I'm at the Olympic Games,* and I get this internal feeling how this program will be, and usually I'm fresh and usually it will be a perfect program. I don't just step out there in training and just say, *Here we go, another program.*

Brian Orser, former world champion in men's figure skating, reflected upon the "feeling" aspect of quality imagery.

■ CORRECTING SKILLS MENTALLY

Sometimes I would think, *Why did I miss that one move? OK, I know what happened, I pulled my body in too close to the apparatus. OK, now how do I avoid that?* Then I try to see myself doing it correctly in imagery. I can actually see the apparatus coming down; I can see the stripe on the club as it rotates, the same way you'd see it when you're doing the routine; that's the best way. Most of the time I look at it from within, because that's the way it's going to be in competition. It is natural because I do the routines so many times that it's drilled into my head, what I see and how I do it. So if I think about a certain part of my club routine, or my ribbon routine, I think of it as the way I've done it so many times, and that's from within my body.

Lori Fung, former Olympic champion in rhythmic gymnastics, used imagery very effectively for skill correction.

With performance imagery, your ultimate goal is to draw on all of your senses to feel yourself executing skills perfectly. This stimulates a slight firing of brain activity and neural pathways that are actually involved in the performance of these skills. It can be viewed as a way of programming your mind and body to execute those skills to perfection. What you are trying to do is program a high-quality performance into your brain and nervous system and to then free your body to follow. Quality imagery helps to establish a positive performance pattern. It also can strengthen your confidence in your ability to perform these skills. Quality mental imagery, combined with quality physical practice, increases your overall effectiveness and brings you closer to your capacity.

The earlier you can begin your imagery training, the better. I recall a very talented eight-year-old gymnast who was capable of incredibly clear imagery. She first began mental imagery completely on her own with no knowledge that it was practiced by many great athletes. She would lie in bed at night running through her routines. For her it seemed a natural thing to do. She was able to see the people around her, feel the moves, and experience the emotions.

I remember a 19-year-old university basketball player who had been experiencing difficulty with a particular play in games. I asked her to try to imagine herself executing the play properly and driving in for a successful layup. She closed her eyes and sat quietly for a couple of minutes. When I asked what had happened in the imagined scene, she said she had seen a bunch of Xs and Os on a chalkboard going through the pattern of the play.

Contrast this with the vivid mental imagery that Bill Russell was doing when he was 18. Russell became one of the best all-time basketball players, winning 11 NBA championships as leader of the Boston Celtics. He describes his use of mental imagery in his book *Second Wind* (Russell 1979, 73-74):

> Something happened that night that opened my eyes and chilled my spine. I was sitting on the bench watching Treu and McKelvey the way I always did. Every time one of them would make one of the moves I liked, I'd close my eyes just afterward and try to see the play in my mind. In other words, I'd try to create an instant replay on the inside of my eyelids. Usually I'd catch only part of a particular move the first time I tried this; I'd miss the headwork or the way the ball was carried or maybe the sequence of steps. But the next time I

saw the move I'd catch a little more of it, so that soon I could call up a complete picture.

On this particular night I was working on replays of many plays, including McKelvey's way of taking an offensive rebound and moving quickly to the hoop. It's a fairly simple play for any big man in basketball, but I didn't execute it well and McKelvey did. Since I had an accurate vision of his technique in my head, I started playing with the image right there on the bench, running back the picture several times and each time inserting a part of me for McKelvey. Finally I saw myself making the whole move, and I ran this over and over. When I went in the game, I grabbed an offensive rebound and put it in the basket just the way McKelvey did. It seemed natural, almost as if I were just stepping into a film and following the signs. When the imitation worked and the ball went in, I could barely contain myself. I was so elated I thought I'd float right out of the gym. Now for the first time I had transferred something from my head to my body. It seemed so easy. My first dose of athletic confidence was coming to me when I was 18 years old.

Being able to picture yourself achieving your goals will help you realize them.

Russell immersed himself in the vivid mental replication of a skilled athlete executing a fast-moving play on the court and driving in for the basket; then he acted out that image. Later he began to create many of his own moves in his mind and played them out on the court.

DEVELOPING YOUR IMAGERY SKILLS

If you have never done any systematic imagery training, start with simple, familiar images or skills. For the next week or two set aside 5 minutes a day, either before going to practice or before going to sleep, to work on your imagery. Let yourself relax. Shut your eyes. (Not yet! First read the next few sentences.) Try to imagine the place where you usually train... what it looks like, how it smells, how it feels when you walk in, the people there, the first things you usually do to warm up, the look and feel of the playing surface and the equipment that you use in your sport. Try to imagine and feel yourself doing some very basic skills in your sport—for example, easy running, free skiing, dribbling, passing, throwing, rolling, swinging, turning, moving freely. Through imagery, gradually increase the complexity of the skills. As a general rule, you should get into a pattern of doing about 10 to 15 minutes of quality imagery every day. Most Olympic and world champions do at least 15 minutes of imagery daily, and many do more when preparing for major competitions.

In addition to helping you perfect physical skills, imagery is a good focusing exercise. You must create and control the images in your mind. It's a mental exercise and it can be tiring, especially in the beginning. So take your time and move into it gradually. It's better to try for short periods of high-quality imagery throughout the day than longer periods of low-quality imagery.

Keep in mind that your ultimate objective is to experience an ideal performance with all your senses. When perfecting performance skills through your imagery, try to call up the feel, not merely something visual. The more vivid and accurate the feeling, and the more effectively you perform within that image, the greater your chances of replicating this image in the real situation. With daily practice, your imagery skills will improve immensely and your imagined performances will feel very real, just as your nighttime dreams feel real.

A good way to perfect feeling-oriented imagery, so critical for excellence in sport, is to integrate a piece of your sport or performance equipment and actually move your body while doing the imagery. Instead of lying down, get into your normal starting position for executing the skill.

For example, a kayak paddler can sit with knees bent and arms up, either holding a paddle or as if holding a paddle, and then actually move her arms through a paddling motion as she imagines and feels her perfect execution in her mind and body. An Alpine skier can assume a standing position (with boots on), leaning slightly forward with knees flexed and arms forward, as if in the starting gate with poles planted. In imagery he then feels himself skiing the course while actually bending his knees and partially moving his body, as if he were actually doing his perfect run. In the quiet of his own apartment or the silence of an empty field, a baseball player can stand up, step into the batter's box, see the windup, swing a real or imaginary bat, and feel the pop of the ball as he imagines and feels his perfect swing. A basketball player can move her body (with or without the ball) and feel perfect shots, beautifully handled passes, and the perfect execution of a variety of offensive and defensive skills. A hockey goalie can put his stick in his hand, stand or sit at the end of the rink, and imagine himself making a series of awesome saves.

When you are learning imagery, movement often helps you call up the total feeling associated with that skill. A gymnast can run through a complete floor routine with feeling by imagining the moves as she walks across the floor doing slight arm movements, body gestures, turns, and pauses. By combining imagery with real movement, you can speed up and enhance the learning process. As you become more skilled at *feeling* imagery, the sensations and emotions associated with great movements will surface more naturally when you imagine and perform your skills.

As you learn to use imagery to perfect old skills or acquire new ones, you might find it helpful to carefully observe others who do those skills exceptionally well. Watch an accomplished athlete perform a skill, and as she is doing it, try to feel yourself doing the skill with her. Do this several times in a row; then try to replay the skill in your own mind, feeling yourself do it. You can use this technique during practices or while viewing videos or competitions.

I once used a video of a world-champion sprinter to help a promising young athlete get the feel of blasting off the blocks and driving through the finish. She watched the video, trying to feel herself go with the image, and then imagined herself moving the same way without the video. She attempted to replicate this feeling of explosive speed, and the specific actions, during her own workout on the track.

Most athletes use imagery primarily as mental preparation for training and competition, as well as for skill correction. Before arriving at the training site, they mentally run through what they want to do and how they want to do it. Just before performing important skills, they imagine themselves doing those skills perfectly, and after errors they imagine themselves making the appropriate corrections before repeating the skills. In preparation for competitions, they mentally run through flawless performances or key parts of their performance. They often imagine themselves in the competitive arena—with the sights, sounds, temperature, spectators, competitors, and coaches—and then focus in on their own performance.

Some of our best athletes have even put a clock on their imagery to ensure that their timing and pacing are exactly what they want. For example, in preparation for the Olympic Games, Alwyn Morris, gold medalist in canoeing, and Alex Baumann, double gold medalist and world record holder in swimming, did timed imagery. Alex Baumann commented:

> The best way I have learned to prepare mentally for competitions is to visualize the race in my mind and to put down a split time. The splits I use in my imagery are determined by my coach and myself, for each part of the race. For example, in the 200 individual medley, splits are made up for each 50 meters because after 50 meters the stroke changes. These splits are based on training times and what we feel I'm capable of doing. In my imagery I concentrate on attaining the splits I have set out to do. About 15 minutes before the race I always visualize the race in my mind and see how it will go. I see where everybody else is, and then I really focus on myself. I do not worry about anybody else. I think about my own race and nothing else. I am really swimming the race in my mind. I go up and down the pool, rehearsing all parts of the race, imagining how I actually feel in the water. I try to get those splits in my mind, and after that I am ready to go. That is what really got me the world record and Olympic medals.

You can use mental imagery to learn new routines, plays, or patterns, and to familiarize yourself with a particular competition site, course, or track. In sports like Alpine skiing, auto racing, cross-country skiing, mountain bike racing and equestrian events, internalizing the course is very important. Our best downhill skiers use imagery extensively to learn the course so that they will be confident in knowing which way to turn when they run the course at 80 miles an hour. During the course inspection, they essentially memorize the course by running it through their minds over and over again. Once all the critical landmarks are known, they imagine themselves skiing the course, seeing and feeling what they will actually experience during the race. Without this mental familiarization process, the risk factor would be dramatically increased, and the confidence a skier needs to really "let it go" in the race would be lacking. Our best cross-country skiers likewise carefully inspect the course, taking note of the difficult parts as well as areas where they can gain ground. This helps them plan strategies and anticipate what they will do at various points in the race (for example, for climbing hills, negotiating sharp downhill turns, and pushing limits).

Many performers find mental imagery helpful to thoroughly evaluate performances and pinpoint important areas for improvement. The process goes something like this: Think of your last performance or game. Mentally replay the highlights—what you did well. What were you focused on when you were doing your best? Then think about parts of your performance that could be improved. Where was your focus when you were doing less than best? Target areas for improvement and imagine yourself making these improvements.

This evaluation process will make you improve more quickly. It can also help you become more aware of how your thinking and focus affect you at different points in the competition. It can lead to a more accurate assessment of what you do or focus on that makes you feel good, perform well, and push your limits. It can also alert you to ways you might be interfering with your own performance and give you specific things to focus on for improvement.

Think about what you can do, or say to yourself, in order to feel better, focus more fully, and perform closer to your capacity. Then begin to practice focusing this way in training, simulations, and in your mental imagery for upcoming competitions.

Mental Rehearsal of Coping Skills

Mentally preparing yourself to cope effectively with distractions, anxiety, or negative thinking is extremely important and yet is largely overlooked in the mental readying process. If in your mind you can see yourself, hear yourself, and feel yourself respond the way you would prefer to respond, you will be better prepared to respond accordingly in the real world. You can mentally rehearse responding appropriately to virtually any situation that might arise, or that you would like to approach in a more positive manner, including a coach screaming at you or a stadium filled with 80,000 people.

Mental rehearsal lets you prepare for and practice effective responses in your mind before you are actually confronted by a real-life challenge, problem, or distraction. It is a buffered kind of learning that can feel real *in your mind* and yet lacks the serious consequences that sometimes occur in the real world. The mental rehearsal process makes it possible to enter a situation feeling better prepared, less fearful, and more confident.

When you think about the attitude and focus that you want to carry into this game or performance, you are mentally preparing yourself to do what you want to do in the real situation. This in itself can help enhance performance and eliminate potential problems that might otherwise affect your performance negatively.

You can imagine yourself at the performance site, feeling positive, saying positive things to yourself, relaxing, overcoming obstacles, focusing only on the task at hand, stretching your limits, achieving your goals. Whatever you want to do, in sport or outside of sport, you can move a step closer to making it a reality by imagining yourself doing it, step-by-step.

A water skier became extremely anxious during important competitions as soon as she passed the first buoy on the way to the slalom run. When she passed this buoy she'd say to herself, *Oh no, here it comes*—and a tenseness would overcome her entire body. She decided to employ mental imagery to practice using the buoy as a signal to relax. She imagined herself skiing by the buoy, saying to herself *Relax,* at which point she would relax her shoulders and think, *You're ready . . . just let it happen.* This process helped her alleviate the problem in the real situation.

A figure skater complained of becoming extremely anxious in important competitions. She was particularly distraught just before starting. She tried to imagine herself at the competition site, from the time she heard her name being called. As the anxious feelings began to surface, she imagined herself relaxing, focused on her breathing, and said to herself, *Nice and smooth . . . flow.* She then imagined herself doing her first few moves in a calm, controlled, and focused manner. She mentally practiced her chosen coping strategy in detail, to feel the effectiveness of her strategy, and to end up focused and in control.

There are many examples of athletes using mental imagery to reduce anxiety, to improve performance, and to cope more effectively with a variety of situations. Some creative uses of imagery were relayed to me by national team archers attending a national training camp. During a workshop I was conducting on mental preparation for shooting, I asked the archers about some of the strategies they had been using. A former world champion spoke of how, through imagery, she was able to transport herself to the world championship from her practice site. Instead of seeing the single target that was actually in front of her, she saw targets stretched across the field. She was fully aware of her competitors. On her right was the leading Polish archer, on her left a German. She could see them, hear them, and feel them. She shot her rounds under these conditions in the same sequence as she would shoot in the real competition. She prepared herself for the competition and distractions by creating the world championships in imagery and by actually shooting under mentally simulated world championship conditions.

A member of the men's national team did just the opposite. In the actual competition he was able to mentally simulate practice conditions. As he prepared to draw his bow to shoot his first arrow at the world championships, his heart was thumping. He glanced down at his tackle box (holding equipment and odds and ends) and noticed the words *Go, go, go,* which one of his hometown buddies had painted in red. That note triggered another reality—a flashback to familiar grounds. From that point on in the competition, he was at home on the practice range, with one small battered target in front of him. He could even hear some of his buddies on the practice field chattering and joking in the background, in place of the chatter of many different nations that surrounded him. He shot in a very steady, collected, and relaxed manner, as if he were at home.

In most cases, mental imagery is a first step in an attempt to improve certain skills or overcome anticipated problems. It gets you started. It is not very time consuming, and you can do it yourself, wherever and whenever you want. Sometimes mental imagery in itself leads to overcoming a particular problem or improving a performance. The usual sequence, however, is to begin with mental imagery, then practice the imagined skill or coping strategy in a real-world training situation, followed by a simulated situation, and finally the event itself. The examples of the two archers who combined simulation and imagery simply point out how you can be very creative in putting together workable strategies.

ADVANCING YOUR IMAGERY

No matter how good or how limited your mental imagery skills are now, you can improve them through daily practice both at home and in your training setting. The more on-site quality imagery you do in your normal practice environment, the more quickly you will improve. If you can imagine the passion and focus you want to bring to today's practice and feel the perfect execution of important skills before you do them in training and competition, this will help you to

- focus on what you want to do,
- remind you of what you need to focus on to do it well,
- improve your imagery skills, and
- set the stage for an improved performance.

Linda Thom, Olympic champion in pistol shooting, commented:

> When I go to the line in training or competition, I mentally go through my shot-plan checklist before I shoot. This strategy started out very mechanically with a physical list of words which I have on the shooting table, and which I read exactly. These words represented every single step involved in shooting a shot. Then I reduced the steps to key words so that I could go through the list faster. Finally, I didn't need a list anymore. I would usually write one word to emphasize what I wanted, such as *trigger* or *smooth*. Then this shot-plan rehearsal became a mix of simple verbal reminders and images, which I ran before each shot.

If you want to develop your imagery to the fullest, try my audiocassette *In Pursuit of Personal Excellence* (see the references and resources section at the end of the book, page 235.)

CHAPTER 10

RELAXATION AND INTENSITY

Performers often fail to achieve their best when they are too tight, anxious, tense, or stressed out. The problem is usually a consequence of losing perspective, task focus, or mental control. Personal bests often occur when mind and muscle combine in free-flowing harmony.

Experiencing high levels of tension and performing in a relaxed, flowing way rarely occur at the same moment. Developing your ability to relax your body and calm your mind is important because it allows you to control your intensity and channel your focus, both of which enhance performance. Relaxation can reduce stress before and during performances and also relieve postevent anxiety and improve general sleeping patterns.

Individuals have different bodily responses to the onset of stress. Some

YOU NEED A CERTAIN AMOUNT OF TENSION TO BE ABLE TO GO. ON THE OTHER HAND, IF YOU ARE TOO FAR GONE, YOU JUST GO OFF THE DEEP END, YOU LOSE CONTROL. SO IT IS JUST BEING ABLE TO FIND THAT LITTLE NARROW COMFORT ZONE.

STEVE PODBORSKI
OVERALL WORLD CUP
DOWNHILL SKI CHAMPION

feel a tenseness in the neck or shoulders. Others experience shaky legs, queasiness in the stomach, a rapid increase in heart rate, sweaty palms, a pounding in the head, and so on. What do *you* feel when you start getting uptight? Stop and think about it. That's a first step to stress control. As you become more fully aware of your early signals of stress, you can use them as cues to relax or shift focus. The trick is to understand your own patterns and to begin to identify and manage them before you get too uptight.

LEARNING TO RELAX

To bring on relaxation, some performers like to focus on relaxing different muscle groups (for example, in the legs, shoulders, arms, or neck) or to focus on breathing slowly and easily, attempting to relax fully with each exhalation. Others like to imagine themselves in a familiar setting with friends or on the beach relaxing as the waves wash gently onto the sandy shore. You may prefer to be alone, talk with others, listen to music, have a massage, seek out a natural outdoor setting; the list goes on. There is no right way to relax. Whatever makes you feel more relaxed and more in control is right for you.

Try to become familiar with different ways of relaxing. Personalize relaxation procedures so that they work best for you. Simple reminders such as *loose, relax,* or *calm* can help relax you instantly if they are well practiced and called upon as soon as you start to feel tense. Self-directed relaxation as well as relaxation assisted by your environments—a long run, a warm bath, a hot shower, a relaxing whirlpool bath, or intimate contact with a loved one—can be helpful in easing you down if anxiety drags on after the event.

Two things happen with effective relaxation. There is a *physiological* relaxation response: your heart slows down, your breathing slows and becomes more regular, your oxygen consumption decreases, your muscles become less tense, and you begin to feel a calmness in your body. There is also a *psychological* relaxation response: a shift in focus to something other than that which caused the increased tension in the first place. Your focus may shift from thoughts about how you are "terrified," or "going to blow it" to simply executing your task or thoughts of your relaxed breathing, the movement of your rib cage, the sensation of specific muscles relaxing, a feeling of calm, the quieting sounds of a song, the beauty in the scenery around you, the pleasant sensations of relaxation, your overall readiness to meet a personal challenge, or your game plan. In short, your focus shifts from fear of failure, fear of rejection, or worry about embarrassing consequences to either relaxation or another constructive focus. The shift away from self-evaluation and worry alone renders you less anxious and puts you more in control; the focus on relaxing your body, executing the next step in your game plan, or doing something joyful further reduces the tension.

I remember one athlete saying to me while going through a relaxation exercise, "I don't need to relax in here; it's out there that I need it." It is out there, when the stress begins to rise, that we all need it. However, if any coping strategy is to be effective under high-stress conditions, it must be well learned and practiced. You must be able to plug in that response in the space of one deep breath. To be able to do this effectively, you have to practice—first under low-stress conditions, then under medium stress, and finally under high-stress conditions. To ready yourself for the competitive arena, you must take advantage of all the stressful situations that you face so that you'll be practiced at responding effectively. Then you will be ready—out there—when you need to be.

If you take the time to learn to relax effectively, you will become more aware of your body's internal environment and better able to adapt to your external environment. It is one way to put yourself more in control.

RELAXATION FOR INDIVIDUAL NEEDS

In my consulting work, many performers have expressed a desire to be able to clear their minds and relax more completely, primarily for the following purposes:

- To fall into a deep and restful sleep, especially before or after an important event, game, or competition
- To remain calm and conserve energy during the final hours leading up to an important performance, game, or competition
- To relax and revitalize the mind and body between different demands, shifts, periods, or events
- To rest and recover while traveling from one game, performance, or meeting, to the next
- To hasten recovery from illness or injury
- To experience more simple joys in life

As a result of those athletes' requests, and with their guidance and feedback, I developed two relaxation tapes that they felt met their individual needs. Each is designed to free the listener to enter a complete state of relaxation—muscle relaxation, relaxed breathing, and relaxation through music and imagery. The script for one relaxation exercise is reproduced at the end of this chapter (pages 131-132). You can make your own tape from this script or listen to one of my cassettes: *In Pursuit of Personal Excellence—Exercises for Concentration and Relaxation* or *Relaxation and Stress Control Activities for Teenagers and Adults*. (See page 236.)

Many performers enjoy and benefit from doing a short relaxation exercise every day, either between practices, work sessions or before going to sleep at night. Whether you use relaxation tapes or follow your own relaxation procedures, try to get totally absorbed in the feeling of relaxation so you can fully benefit from it and so that you can recall that feeling in the future. If your goal is to develop your ability to call upon a relaxation response quickly in a stressful setting, then conclude the relaxation session by repeating to yourself a reminder word, such as *relax, breathe,* or *loose* every time you exhale. This is meant to strengthen the association between your reminder and total relaxation in your body. Then begin to think of your reminder and recall the feeling of relaxation in other settings. Let the relaxed feeling flow quickly through your body. The process goes something like this.

Think to yourself: *breathe, relax, calm, let go, loose.* Let that peaceful, relaxed sensation spread throughout your body. Then scan your body for any areas of tension. Some people find it helpful to imagine a beam of light scanning the body. The light beam is charged with relaxation, so if any area of tension exists, one simply zaps it with a beam of relaxation.

Experiment with this process first in a quiet setting, and then start to do it in other settings. In the beginning, you may need a couple of minutes to feel completely relaxed. Your goal is to be able to bring on a relaxation response within one breath or a few seconds.

Try using your reminder to relax while sitting, standing, walking, running, talking, reading, driving, in school, at work, at meetings, at workouts, on the beach, in bed, and so on.

You can start right now. Breathe in . . . breathe out . . . say to yourself, *re-lax . . . re-lax . . . re-lax.* Now scan your body for any areas of tension. Are your shoulders relaxed? Is your jaw relaxed? These are often good checkpoints. Zap any area of tension with a beam of relaxation. Set a goal for yourself to relax on the spot five times today. You've already done it once—four more to go. Next, start plugging your relaxation response into potentially anxiety-provoking situations. If competition has resulted in unwanted tension, then begin to simulate competitive conditions in practice and use your cue to relax. Move from simulated conditions to actual competitive conditions, from less important competitions to more important ones. This allows your on-site relaxation response to become well learned and practiced for those times when you need it most.

Taking an exam, participating in a tryout, speaking in class, going to the dentist, having an argument, responding to a customs official, or getting a parking ticket—all provide valuable practice opportunities. As soon as you detect any of your personal signals of tension, take a deep breath, exhale slowly, and think to yourself, *re-lax, calm.* With practice, this in itself can bring on a relaxation response. It is not likely that relaxation alone will eliminate anxiety entirely in a highly stressful situation, but it should help you reduce it to a manageable level and allow you to regain a more constructive focus.

Relaxation can reduce stress and enhance recovery before, during, and after performances.

RELAXING THROUGH EXERTION

When Florence Griffith-Joyner blitzed the women's 100-meter world record in 10.48 seconds at the 1988 Olympic Trials, she commented, "The 10.60 [run in the first round of the competition] made me realize if I continued to concentrate on what I'm doing and stay relaxed, my times would continue to drop." And they did!

Sue Holloway, following her Olympic silver medal performance kayaking in pairs, spoke of the importance of relaxing:

■ Almost every three seconds or so toward the end I'd have to say *relax*, and I'd let my shoulders and my head relax, and I'd think about putting on the power, and then I'd feel the tension creeping up again so I'd think about relaxing again, then *power, relax.* . . . I knew that in order to have that power I had to be relaxed. You can be powerful but tense, and the boat won't go. You windmill and you stay on the spot and dig yourself into a hole. I wanted to feel the power, the boat coming up, lifting and going. Crossing the line, the thing I remember was just letting the emotion go and being able to say, *That's it, it's over!* I just knew that we'd gone our very hardest.

At first glance, exertion and relaxation may seem to be a contradiction in terms. However, most best performances in sport occur when athletes feel loose and relaxed in the process of extending themselves. When Larry Cain paddled at a blistering pace to win Olympic gold, there was a definite sequence of reach–power–relax with each stroke. He pushed his limits, but he also paddled relaxed. With top runners you see a similar sequence of stretch–power–relax accompanying each stride. They often speak of running relaxed after shattering world records. When you watch cheetahs run at speeds approaching 80 miles an hour, you see that they also run with beautiful, relaxed power.

To develop the skills that allow you to relax during exertion, set a goal to work on this during training sessions, and then remind yourself to relax while you are going hard in training. Think of on-site reminders that might help you get into a relaxed but highly focused channel (for example, *loose–powerful; power–relax; reach–pull–relax; stretch–grab–relax*). Experiment with calling on reminders at appropriate times before and during workouts. In activities that involve repetitive sequences, reminders can be timed to go with the rhythmical flow of the activity.

Marathon runners would not be breaking personal barriers, some by running 26 miles in times ranging from 2 hours and 6 minutes to 2 hours and 10 minutes, unless they were stretching, pushing, reaching, and relaxing through their limits. The best distance runners run relaxed, breathe steadily and consistently, relax muscles with periodic exhalation, scan muscles for tension, and focus on localized relaxation of tense areas. They use only those muscles required, relax nonessential muscles (including jaw and shoulder muscles), and relax working muscles in the recovery stage to conserve energy and run more efficiently. You can learn to relax your nonworking muscles while other muscles are working hard and to relax your working muscles in the recovery phase of sequential movements. You will do this effectively only if you focus on doing it in training. You know where all those muscles are; you simply have to practice tuning in to them and telling them what to do at critical moments.

By relaxing and by focusing on specific functions within your own body, you can effect physiological changes in your muscle tension, blood pressure, respiratory rate, blood flow, and body temperature, and even influence your rate of recovery from injury. When attempting to direct such changes, clearly visualize the part of the body that you want to influence, then feel the desired change taking place. There is a chapter (Create a Strong Mind-Body Connection, chapter 7) on enhancing your own healing, which includes practical exercises, in my book *Embracing Your Potential: Steps to Self-Discovery, Balance, and Success in Sports,Work and Life.* (See references and resources, page 235, for details).

MAINTAINING INTENSITY

A Chinese coach once said to me, "You can jump over a very high fence when a big bull is chasing you." I haven't tried that one yet, but I think it would give me a little lift. Being pumped up or energized can help you achieve greater heights, as long as you channel that energy in the right direction. But in your haste, you wouldn't want to trip and fall before you reach the fence, or run into it rather than going up and over.

You might be naturally up before important games or competitions, and not require anything additional to heighten your precompetition intensity. If you do need a lift, it will likely be when fatigue begins to set in toward the latter part of the game, race, or performance—when every stroke, every movement, every inch counts. This is when a charging bull or another effective way of energizing may be most helpful.

Being able to maintain optimal intensity and full focus for the duration of the game or performance is the goal of many great performers. This often separates great performances from lesser performances, winning teams from losing teams.

The challenge is to discover how to attain and maintain that ideal level of focus and intensity, not only for the duration of one shift, period, game, or performance, but over the course of a season or career. There are two important parts to maintaining a high level of intensity—what you do with your focus on-site and what you do to recharge your batteries away from the performance arena.

What works best for you to enter and maintain a high level of focused intensity? If you hope to perform closer to your potential consistently or even once, this is something you will have to discover and work on. Many different approaches can work to bring a delicious intensity to your pursuits, and what works best may change over time. However, I have discovered that the heart of intensity among the great athletes I have worked with is quite basic. They simply *decide* to go out there and play with full intensity and full focus—every second. They make that commitment to themselves before every game, every period, every shift. Intensity is a decision, because we are all capable of bringing a certain level of intensity to our pursuits and relaxing outside the performance arena. Great performers make a commitment to themselves to relax and rest well away from the performance site so that they have the energy required to play and focus with a high level of intensity from the first second to the last.

Fear is sometimes used to increase intensity—fear of failure, fear of embarrassment, fear of being cut from the team. Fear can heighten intensity, but it can also paralyze performers—when they lose their best performance focus or become too tense, tentative, and fearful of making a mistake. Performing well or winning may result in increased intensity, but it can also result in complacency. The same is true with losing. So much depends on how you perceive the situation and how you channel your thoughts and focus.

One way to maintain high levels of focus and intensity over time, through the ups and downs is to draw upon your positive emotions and the passion you have for your pursuit. Think about positive possibilities, personal bests, past and future contributions, highlights, positive opportunities, and the possibility of making a difference every day, every shift, every step. It is extremely important to find ways of keeping the pride, passion, joy, and excitement in your daily pursuits.

What often works best in times of low intensity or fatigue *during* performances is a shift in focus *away* from the fatigue to technical or task reminders that help you perform better—*jump, pull, reach, extend, follow through*—or to reminders that help energize you— *commit, strong, go, charge, power, push, quick, explode now.* For some sports, reminders can be repeated in a rhythmical fashion; for others, a single crisp action thought is more appropriate. Another way to increase your intensity is to remind yourself of your goal and the importance of achieving it: *I've invested too much to give up now. It won't kill me. I want to do it.* Do it now—don't finish the game or performance knowing you could have given more. Shift your focus back to the doing, in the present—giving it everything you have.

To relax in stressful situations, play down the importance of outcome, slow down your pre-event pace, breathe easily and slowly, let your body move freely. Focus on your pre-event preparation and only on what you are doing. If you need a wake-up call to raise your level of intensity, remind yourself of the importance of this event— how much you have invested, how much others have invested, and how much depends on what you do. Draw upon powerful positive emotions, including thoughts about the great things you have done or can do. Increase the speed and physical intensity of your warm-up. Do short bursts of high-intensity activity at maximum effort, jump up and down, listen to inspiring music. All of these simple actions can increase your overall level of intensity—especially if you are feeling flat.

It is interesting to note that athletes who consistently maintain high-intensity focus or effort for the duration of the performance or game are also the ones who bring high intensity and focus to everyday practices. Practicing with focused intensity establishes a positive pattern of performing that is naturally carried into games and performances. This is one reason that high-quality, high-intensity practice is so important. The more players on a team who are able to generate and maintain a high level of intensity throughout the game, the better that team will perform.

By setting specific practice goals and thinking about how you will achieve these goals on the way to practice, you can generate focus and intensity in situations where you otherwise might feel bored or unchallenged. Creating competitive challenges in practice can also raise the level of intensity. For example, you could hold scrimmages; compete against teammates or the clock; train with outside athletes; or bring in officials, judges, or spectators. Some of our best athletes use competition against opponents of lesser or greater skill as a challenge to meet personal performance goals and as an opportunity to practice their competitive moves in preparation for more important events.

Perhaps most important is deciding for yourself that you are going to bring intensity and focus to practice and committing yourself to do it—every day. Commit to performing in practice with focus and intensity. This will make a huge difference in your performance. If you don't train with focus and intensity, somebody else will—and that will give them an advantage. The rare times that I feel it is not a good idea to bring physical intensity to practices is if you are recovering from an injury, or if you are sick or are extremely fatigued—for example, in the middle of a long, hard season that has included extensive travel. In these cases, it is often best to take time off or to do light, low-intensity training because you will benefit more from rest than from hard exertion.

It is important for you to discover the level of intensity that is most appropriate for you to perform your best in your sport or performance domain. Then practice getting into that zone and maintaining it, so that becomes your natural way of performing. To know how is not enough; to put it into action and maintain it when and where you need it is the goal. You can do this with planning and practice.

RELAXATION EXERCISE

This three-part relaxation exercise is designed to free you to enter a state of complete relaxation through muscle relaxation, relaxed breathing, and imagery.[1] If you want to use the exercise to go to sleep, remind yourself before you begin listening that you will allow yourself to fall into a deep and restful sleep.

To use the exercise as a lead-in to performance imagery, remind yourself before you begin listening that at the conclusion of the exercise, while you are still in a deeply relaxed state, you will imagine and feel preselected performance skills flowing perfectly in your mind and body.

If you want to use the exercise to calm yourself before an important competition, select an appropriate time to listen—a time when you would prefer to be more relaxed and when you do not yet need to be highly activated for competing.

To use the exercise as a lead-in to strengthening your confidence, remind yourself before you listen that at the conclusion of the exercise you will repeat to yourself your many assets, your strengths, and your many reasons to be positive and confident in yourself and your capacity. You might want to write down some positive statements to think about before you begin the relaxation exercise.

If your objective is to heal your body or speed your recovery from a strenuous or stressful day, then prepare yourself to send healing thoughts and revitalizing images to various parts of your body—both during and after the relaxation exercise.

RELAXATION SCRIPT

Get yourself into a comfortable position. Let yourself relax. Feel the relaxation spread through your body. Breathe easily and slowly. Become aware of your feet. Move your toes slightly. Let them relax. Now think into your lower legs. Let your calf muscles totally relax. Think into your upper legs. Let them totally relax. Feel your legs sink into a completely relaxed state. Relax your behind.

[Pause]

Focus on the muscles in your lower back. Think relaxation into those muscles. Feel that relaxation spread into your upper back. Feel your whole body sink into a deep state of relaxation. Now focus on your fingers. Feel them tingle slightly. Think warmth into your fingers. Let them totally relax. Relax your forearms, your upper arms, and your shoulders. Totally relax. Relax your neck [pause] and your jaw. Feel your head sink into a totally relaxed and comfortable position.

Scan your body for possible areas of tightness and relax those areas. Feel your entire body encircled with soothing warmth and relaxation. Enjoy this wonderful state of complete relaxation.

[Pause for one minute]

Now focus on your breathing. Breathe easily and slowly.

[Pause]

As you breathe in, allow your stomach to rise and extend. As you breathe out, let your whole body relax. Breathe in—feel your stomach rise. Breathe out—relax. Breathe in—feel your stomach rise. Breathe out—relax. [Do three times.] For the next 10 breaths, each time you breathe in feel your stomach rise— each time you breathe out think to yourself . . . relax . . . relax . . . relax.

[Pause 10 breaths]

Feel yourself sink deeper and deeper into a calm and wonderful state of complete relaxation.

Now in your mind you are going to a very special place. You can go here whenever you want to find peace and tranquility. In your special place the sun is shining. The sky is blue. You are totally relaxed, enjoying the warmth and tranquility.

[Pause]

Feel the warmth. Enjoy the beauty.

[Pause]

You can be here alone or you can share this place with a special friend. It is your place. You decide.

In your special place, it is so relaxing. You are calm, relaxed, confident, and happy to be alive. You are in control. You feel great.

Feel the calmness spread through your entire body and mind as you rest gently, enjoying the peace and tranquillity of your special place. You are feeling so good and so relaxed. You are comfortable, you are warm, you are safe. You are in control of your body and mind. Enjoy this wonderful, restful state.

---

[1]Available on the audiocassette *In Pursuit of Personal Excellence,* available from Orlick Excel, CP 1807, Chelsea, QC, Canada J9B 1A1

CHAPTER 11

DISTRACTION CONTROL

If I were asked to choose one mental skill that distinguishes athletes and other performers who remain at the top of their game, I would name their ability to adapt and refocus in the face of distractions. If you want to perform near your best consistently, you must develop the critical skill of distraction control through regular practice. You must learn to hold your best focus in the face of potential distractions, and to refocus effectively to quickly regain the connection if it is broken.

Distractions come from a variety of sources: winning; losing; the expectations of others; your own expectations; family members; relationships; teammates; coaches; supervisors; competitors; scores; officials; media; sponsors; financial and educational concerns; changes in your own performance level; fatigue;

HEART IN CHAMPIONS HAS TO DO WITH THE DEPTH OF YOUR MOTIVATION AND HOW WELL YOUR MIND AND BODY REACT TO PRESSURE—THAT IS, BEING ABLE TO DO WHAT YOU DO BEST UNDER MAXIMUM PAIN AND STRESS.

BILL RUSSELL
WINNER OF 11 NBA
CHAMPIONSHIPS

injury; illness; extra demands; changes in familiar patterns; and your own thinking before, during, and after performances. Distractions are an ever-present, ongoing part of sport and life.

When you enter competitive situations or demanding work environments, the number of potential distractions increases substantially. However, you decide whether you let these things distract you, upset you, lower your confidence, put you in a negative frame of mind, take you out of your best focus, or interfere with your performance

It is your choice, because something becomes a distraction only if you let it distract you. Otherwise, it is simply something that happens as you go through your day, your preparation, your competition, or your performance. You can choose to be distracted by it or not to be distracted, to dwell on it or to let it go.

The most important point is that you don't have to let what you normally think of as a distraction affect your mood or performance in a negative way. You don't lose your performance skills because of distractions; you let yourself lose the focus that allows you to execute your skills effectively. You may not like what someone says or does, but you don't have to react with anger or lose emotional control. You may be faced with a decision, judgment, or rule that you feel is unfair, but you don't have to let it destroy your performance or your day. Parts of your performance or life may not go as smoothly as you wish on a particular day; you may find that frustrating, but you are not obliged to react by putting yourself or others down, giving up, or questioning your own capacity. There may be disruptions that you did not expect—such as schedule changes; additional demands; delays; incompetent people; lack of personal space; or differences in facilities, accommodations, or food. You still don't have to be overcome by those events or let your positive focus slip away. You may want a good result more than anything else, but you don't have to react by overthinking, overanalyzing, or worrying about the outcome. You can simply remind yourself to focus in a way that will allow you to perform your best given the conditions you are facing.

You can find a way over, around, or through almost all obstacles by committing yourself to remain positive, by turning negatives into positives, by drawing out lessons and regaining a fully connected focus as quickly as possible. When reacting emotionally to distractions or potential obstacles, you defeat yourself because it takes away your best performance focus, and leaves you mentally and physically drained. If you continue to react in this way over a long period of time or throughout an event that lasts for a period of days or weeks—like many tournaments or championships—you risk not only becoming exhausted, but also getting sick. Constantly reacting to potentially stressful situations in a negative way takes a lot of energy and lowers your resistance. This obviously can hurt your performance and add still another stress factor.

When you are going to face additional stress, additional rest is a blessing. If you are well rested, you will cope better with stress. It's important, too, to rest *after* stress. Setting simple daily goals and planning each day to ensure you get some rest, do something you enjoy, and gain some sense of control over what you do is very helpful in stressful environments.

At major competitions, in demanding performance situations, or ongoing interpersonal relationships, if you step back and look at distractions from a distance, as I often do, you realize that most of them are little things that get resolved within a short time. They really aren't worth wasting your emotional energy on.

The following pointers will help you stay on track or get back on track quickly:

- Commit yourself to remaining positive.

- Focus on doing what will help you stay positive and in control. A strong positive focus protects you from distractions.

- Get yourself into a positive state of mind before the event, and stay focused on your job within the event; then things will flow.

- Look for advantages in every possible situation, even if the conditions are less than ideal. Look for reasons why you can still be positive, confident, strong, and optimistic.

- Find the positives in the situations you are experiencing or in which you are currently living.

- Remind yourself that distractions do not have to absorb you. You can refuse to get caught up in them. You can let them go. At a tournament, competition, or performance site things may happen to you that are unfair, unexpected, or beyond your control, but you can control how you react to those things. It is useless to drag yourself down or waste energy trying to control things that are beyond your control. Why compound the problem by focusing good energy on things that are beyond your immediate control?

- Expect conditions to be different at important events or major competitions. Expect a faster pace, a busier place, and more waiting around. Prepare yourself to face these potential distractions in a positive way. Let them go with as little energy as possible. They are not worth your reaction. Let them bounce off you easily.

• Expect people to behave differently at stressful events, even those who normally would be calm, supportive, and understanding. Observe them with interest, but don't take responsibility for their behavior. Look for your own strength. Remind yourself of where your focus should be.

• Know that you can enjoy the experience and perform well, regardless of the circumstances. Distraction control can be a valuable asset in all parts of your life. In preparing yourself to make positive thinking a way of being, consider the following pointers:

• Practice getting back on track. For example, when things don't go well in training, while performing, or in your personal life, take advantage of the opportunity to practice refocusing into a more positive state of mind. Turn bad moods into good moods. Then you will be prepared for your most important challenges in sport and life.

• Make a real effort to remain positive. Focus on doing the things that are most likely to keep you in a positive frame of mind. Find your own space, regroup your thoughts, pursue things that are meaningful for you, know that it is not worth wasting energy on hassles, focus on aborbing yourself in something that is interesting or beautiful or joyful. Challenge yourself to think and act in positive, self-enhancing ways, especially when things are not going well. Remind yourself repeatedly that you can change your focus and perspective.

• Do what you can do—learn from it, then move on. Focus on what is within your control.

• After a good day or a not-so-good day, be proud of your effort and of what you have done well and draw out the positive lessons. Then start a fresh, new day.

To protect themselves from unwanted stress or distractions at the performance site, some performers find it helpful to imagine themselves surrounded by an invisible bubble or force field. This force field allows you your needed personal space and shields you from intrusions or potentially harmful input. Negative comments, distractions, or hassles simply bounce off your protective shield as you move toward your goal; only positive things come through.

Your best on-site focus is usually limited to preparation for your own performance—something over which you have control. Focus on following your own preferred preparation patterns. Focus on what you want to do and how you plan to do it—not on others or distractions. Think only of what focus works best for you; it has worked well in the past. Bring yourself into this frame of mind—it is the only place to be. You are not asking yourself to do anything unreasonable, only to perform as you can perform. The doing is your goal. Execute your task the way it can be done, the way you can do it. Feel it. Your body cooperates with your thoughts and images when you send a clear message and then just let it happen. Trust your preparation; trust your body. Let it happen by instinct. Focus ahead and go. Let your body lead.

Performing your best requires distraction control.

TRAINING TO REFOCUS

Think of a recent situation in work, practice, competition, or daily life where you lost it—blew your cool, lost your temper, abandoned your positive focus, or lost your connection with your performance. Can you recall that scene in your mind? How could you have responded more effectively? Now, imagine that you are confronted with the same situation, but you don't let it bother you. You rise above it. It bounces off you with minimal disturbance. You stay cool and get back on track quickly. You remain positive, calm, controlled, focused, and effective. How can you get yourself to do that?

First, you need a plan that outlines how you would prefer to respond in this situation. Then you can imagine yourself responding more effectively in that situation or other situations that you have already faced. This will help set the stage for improving your refocusing skills. You then have to practice your positive refocusing plan in real situations in the real world.

The next time something goes wrong—a negative comment, a missed move, too much thinking, a loss of focus—challenge yourself to turn it around within that setting or training session. Set a goal to regain your positive focus or total connection with your performance, and to do it as quickly as possible.

The next time you are about to get upset or slip into a bad mood because of your reaction to someone, or something that happened in a relationship, concentrate on regaining a positive focus or a focus that reconnects you in a positive way. This is a true challenge. If it were easy, everyone would be great at it—but few of us are. And we would all live in complete harmony with our loved ones and perform to our fullest capacity under high-stress conditions—but few of us do. Nevertheless, it is possible to make significant improvements in our ability to focus in more positive ways if we make this our daily goal, and whenever we are successful, make a note of how we achieved it.

■ CHANGING FOCUS

Sylvie Bernier began to work seriously on distraction control about one and a half years before the Olympics. Previously she had suffered from distractions that resulted in inferior performances, especially on the last dives of the competition. Sylvie's main distraction was paying attention to the scoreboard (leaderboard) instead of focusing on her own dives.

I started to shift away from the scoreboard a year and a half before the Olympics because I knew that every time I looked at the scoreboard, my heart went crazy. I couldn't control it. I knew that I dove better if I concentrated on my diving instead of concentrating on everyone else. It was harder to get ready for 10 dives than for 1 dive, so I decided to stop looking at everyone else, just be myself and focus on preparing for my next dive. That was the best way for me to concentrate for my event. Between dives at a meet, using a Walkman was the best way for me to shut everything out. I knew I could win, but I had to dive well. I stopped saying, "This diver's doing this, so she's going to miss this one," or "If she misses one, I'm going to win."

At the Olympics I really focused on my dives instead of on other divers. That was the biggest change in those two years. Before that, I used to just watch the event and watch the Chinese, and think, *Oh, how can she do that? She's a great diver.* Then I thought, *I'm as good as anyone else, so let's stop talking about them and focus on your own dives.* That was an important step in my career.

■ RECOVERING FROM SETBACKS

If you have a bad routine, you've got to get back to zero again. You just have to say, *OK, that's forgotten. It's totally forgotten.* That's it. Go out and do the next one, and pretend that the next one is the first routine of the day and it is going to count. Otherwise, you are never going to pull back again. You can't do anything about it. You can't do anything about the score you're getting. You can't do anything about why you dropped that one move or how great it was; it's over and done with. Sometimes it's really hard to make yourself forget it, but the more you try, the better you're going to get at it in the future.

> *Lori Fung, Olympic champion in rhythmic gymnastics, discussing the importance of refocusing between events, especially after an error.*

■ KEEPING YOUR FOCUS

Once I push out at the start, I am focused on where I am at the time. A lot of it is "line" in downhill. You don't go right at the gate, you've got the line that you have been running all week and you just say, *Okay, I've got to stay high here, I have to go direct here, I have to jump this jump,* just so I am aware of each obstacle as it comes. If I make a small mistake, often it doesn't even register for me until the end, when I'm at the bottom. At the time you are still thinking *forward, speed, momentum.* You don't carry the mistake down the hill. It is shelved until later. Often those mistakes will mean just running them out, and it really won't cost you that much time if you don't panic, if you just let it turn out and get back on track.

Laurie Graham, winner of many World Cup races in downhill skiing, reflecting on her way of staying focused within a race.

Focusing through distractions is probably the most important skill of all for consistently performing to your potential in your most important challenges or competitions. It is a skill that needs a lot of practice to be perfected.

What focus do you want to carry today? Think about it. Make it clear in your mind. Know that you can make it happen. You have the capacity to live that focus today. Take control. *Make it happen.*

CHAPTER 12

SIMULATION

Simulation training lets you practice your desired performance responses and coping strategies in circumstances that are as real as you can make them before you take them into the real situation. Test pilots and astronauts were among the first to use simulation training effectively. In preparation for a space voyage, astronauts take great care to simulate every potential condition that they could experience in space—including the launch, all in-flight and surface activities, and many possible malfunctions, along with appropriate responses for each. The cost of error is high when human life and billions of dollars are at stake, so no effort is spared to ensure that the astronauts are as well prepared as possible for their mission—without yet having ventured into space on that mission. Before they leave the

TO HAVE BEEN THERE BEFORE WITHOUT EVER HAVING BEEN THERE—THAT IS THE GOAL OF SIMULATION.

launch pad, they feel totally ready—as if they have been there before, knowing that they can perform effectively and handle any problems that arise.

Astronaut Chris Hadfield described the importance of simulation training:

> We simulate a tremendous amount in preparation for space flight and we try to make our simulations and our simulators as realistic as possible. We work very hard to set up a scenario that is realistic, that is credible, so the people in the shuttle simulator feel like they're in a shuttle, the people in mission control feel like they're controlling a real shuttle. So there's a lot of air of realism to it. Then we will set up the malfunctions so that you drive the system to its edges, try and get into a gray area. What if this failed and this failed? Do our rules cover us? Would we know what to do? And so we try and drive ourselves to the edge, and hopefully during the simulation we'll get into a situation that we've never been in before and figure our way through it. We also debrief in exhaustive detail. The way it runs is the person who was running the simulation, the flight director or the shuttle commander, has kept major event notes through the whole exercise, whether it's 4 hours or an 8-hour simulation or a 36-hour simulation, whatever. They will hit every single major event during the simulation and what went right, thank the people that did it right, or if there was a new way of doing something that worked better, and then definitely get into the details of what went wrong or what was inefficient. Then actions are taken to put that into the flight rules or put that into the training from now on. Let's expand our collective brain power here. Let's learn from this thing.
>
> We've gotten to the point now where we've flown the shuttle over 90 times and we've made it look effortless. That is purely through accurate simulation and then incredible attention to detail in learning every lesson you can from every effort and rolling that back into the training flow so that the next one is even better, or optimized. We implement things as quickly as possible. If it's something that is critical, we'll turn it around in a day, put it in the simulator, run it, and come out with the change the next day. For my first mission I would guess we did an actual full crew simulation of the docking (with the space station) 250 times. And then myself simulating stages of it, or complete bits of it in my head, I couldn't count the number of times. I sat out on my deck

at home, at night, and thought through it and practiced with it. When we actually got to do it, it was easy because of our detailed planning and detailed preparation.

The most important thing in the training is to have representative, environmentally situated training, enough training that when you get to the real test that you have seen something that was close enough or you have been able to extrapolate to it so that it becomes familiar. So you aren't relying on chance when it really comes down to it, so that it becomes familiar and you can just focus down and get this job done and it's within the scope of what you've seen before.

In sport, simulation training can help prepare you to more effectively meet the challenges that you will face. Simulation prepares you physically and technically through the high-quality, high-intensity training that replicates the demands of competition. It helps you prepare mentally for competition conditions and potential distractions so that you are better able to stay focused and get the job done regardless of the demands of your event or the happenings around you.

WHO USES SIMULATION?

In the 1988 Winter Olympics, professional figure skater Elizabeth Manley delivered her best-ever international performance, winning the long program and placing second overall. She previously had experienced problems with her long program and often worried before competing about whether she could get through a clean program. To perform to her capacity at the Olympics, she needed to feel confident that she could skate the whole program with no problems and to know that she could maintain total focus on executing her skills. To fully prepare herself, Liz did more complete run-throughs of her program that year than she had ever done before. In her final simulations, which took place in an arena similar in size to the Olympic arena, she imagined that she was skating at the Olympics. Liz was very confident going into her long program at the Olympics, and she executed a flawless program. The additional simulations had really helped.

Eric Heiden won five gold medals in speed skating at the 1980 Winter Olympics. Speed skating is a high-intensity sport that involves a lot of pain when you are going flat-out. To excel in a sport like this, you must somehow learn how to push through pain barriers. Toward the end of many events like this, your muscles are hurting, burning, screaming.

Fortunately, the pain experienced by most well-conditioned athletes as they extend limits is simply the sign of a sane body talking to its seemingly insane master: "What are you doing to me? I'm wiped out, my muscles are reaching a point of extreme fatigue. I've had enough pounding for one day. Can't we stop?" *No, we can't stop. I'm the master here and we have to continue, but it won't be long now . . . only another few strokes, another few steps. Anyway, it's not actually pain; it's just the feeling you get when your muscles are really working.*

"That's easy for you to say, tucked away up there, sitting safely in your skull. Why don't you come down here and try pushing a little weight?" And so the debate continues. But this is a battle the mind must win over the body, because in many events you must push past the pain barrier to explore your limits. Most of us can tolerate higher levels of discomfort—if we are comforted by knowing that it is helping us achieve our goal, and that we can always stop it if we choose to.

Eric Heiden often used simulation training to practice pushing through personal barriers. He even included the pain in his mental imagery of races, and in his mind raced beyond the pain. He pushed through discomfort barriers so often in training that he was totally prepared to endure and extend limits in major competitions. Sometimes he pushed so hard in training that his legs were too shaky to stand. Like Eric, speed skater Gaetan Boucher trained with incredible intensity and used simulation training extensively in preparation for his double gold medal performance at the Olympics.

If you replicate competition demands in training, you will simply be much better prepared to perform to your capacity in the real situation. However, it is important to realize that you can't train with that intensity every day or every interval. Even though you need to find ways of pushing limits or replicating competition demands on a regular basis, rest is equally essential. You need to be physically and mentally rested to get the best out of yourself in major simulations and major competitions.

Many adverse or unforeseen conditions can be prepared for and overcome if similar conditions have already been simulated in practice. Performing under simulated adverse conditions is one way of knowing that you can do well under all kinds of circumstances. By foreseeing and working through possible problem situations, you can enter them with less fear and more confidence. Simulation helps you to do what you are capable of doing—because you know what to do and know you can do it.

If something does go wrong, you can move right through it. It's unfortunate, but no big deal: *I can adapt and still perform well. I can perform well with a brief warm-up or even a poor warm-up, whether we are up or down, on target or slightly off target. I can perform well with announcements or other distractions going on right in the middle of my performance or mission. I'm in control here. I have my skills. All I have to do is focus on doing them.*

Real-world simulation prepares you to overcome all kinds of potential distractions. Think of the kinds of things that happen or might happen in big meets or key games or on important missions. Introduce them into your practice setting. Some things that cannot be replicated in practice can be simulated through mental imagery, so at least you have worked through an effective response in your mind.

Introduce the expected. Enter the gym or arena, warm up, and play your game or run through your events just as you would in competition. Bring in judges, officials, cameras, and, where possible, athletes to compete with. Run through your event, program, or game in uniform, in the rain, in the sun, in the heat, in the cold, when tired, when fresh, after eating, after missing a meal, in the morning, in the afternoon, in the evening. Practice overcoming difficult offenses and defenses, false starts, someone passing you on the inside late in the run, coming off the bench, or coming on strong toward the final three quarters of the race or game even though you have slipped behind. Introduce sounds of applause or PA announcements just when you are beginning an approach or are halfway through a routine. Warm up on your own and run through your events on your own, without your coach being there (your coach may be stuck in traffic or delayed at a meeting).

Have your coach, close friends, or other athletes introduce some expected "unexpected" changes that you must adapt to. For example, the coach (or a friend role-playing the coach) can tell you that you have an hour to warm up, only to start the competition in 15 minutes instead; she can change the lineup, offense, defense, or order of events at the last minute; she can bring in judges, unfair officials, important evaluators, cameras, lights, and so on. You can practice being calm, focused, and in control under all these simulated conditions. Before introducing these kinds of procedures to prepare you

Simulation training can prepare you for the expected *and* unexpected and help you achieve your goals.

for potential distractions, the overall rationale for doing so should be discussed openly among athletes and coaches.

A young figure skater found that while she was waiting to perform in competitions, she often became aware of other skaters coming off the ice saying, "It is so hot out there . . . it is so hard to get through." As she stepped on the ice herself, she worried about the heat and about how it would affect her performance. During the final minute of her five-minute program, she was thinking, *It's so hot . . . my mouth is so dry . . . feels like there's no air . . . I don't think I am going to get through to the end.* In her last competition she barely scraped through the last portion of her program and was not at all pleased with her performance. Interestingly, she never worried about the heat in practice meets or exhibitions. It only happened in competitions, even though the physical setup in exhibitions was basically the same: packed arena, bright lights, and high temperature. This led me to believe that the young skater's anxiety about performing well in the heat of competition was raised more by the other skaters' comments about the heat than the heat itself.

We discussed the possibility of practicing with an elevated arena temperature. This posed some logistical problems, so we decided to try increasing the skater's body temperature and leaving the rink manager's body temperature alone. We agreed that at the next practice, she would dress very warmly in heavy clothing and then try running through her full free program.

She reported back a few days later and said, "I did my program in practice with a big sweater and leg warmers. I was burning hot, but I didn't have a problem with it. I didn't even think about it." From that time on, heat was no longer a major problem in her competitions. Even if all the other skaters came off the ice complaining about the heat, she was never preoccupied with it. She really just needed to know that she could handle the situation without a problem—which she could. The simulation merely provided a little confidence-enhancing proof.

All performers gain from having confidence in their ability to do what they are capable of doing. Many would like to enter performances or competitions knowing in advance they will get through their programs or perform to their capacity. Simulation helps build this confidence. It sometimes helps to do more in your simulations than you are required to do in your competitions. For example, if you know that one five-minute performance program will be required, do two in a row; if you know that your game will last an hour, play an additional half hour of high-intensity overtime.

Obviously, you must build up your performance level by setting progressively more challenging goals, and by being well rested on the days that you choose to do these kinds of simulations. However, once you are used to doing more than is required, doing what is required is no big deal. If you are accustomed to playing four or five periods of fully focused high-intensity hockey in simulated competitive games, you should be able to enter the competitive arena with full confidence in your ability to maintain your focus and intensity for the mere three periods. Top Asian gymnasts have used this approach successfully. I have seen them execute two complete routines in a row before dismounting. This is one reason their routines are so flawless in competition. The knowledge that in practice they regularly do more than the competition demands gives them full confidence that they can hit clean routines.

You (and your coach) are in the best position to determine what kinds of simulated conditions might be most relevant and helpful in your sport or performance domain. The important point is that if you have been exposed to most of the expected and unexpected conditions that are likely to occur at major events or competitions, you will be better equipped to stay focused and to perform your best under these conditions. If you have practiced doing more than is required, you will feel more prepared. You will know you can do well. No sweat. Well, some sweat—but you'll know you can nail it. Simulation gives you added confidence in your ability to do what you set out to do. It helps you believe in yourself, and that is crucial in all sports and on all missions. Your objective is to reach the point where you can face all kinds of challenges or distractions and still have confidence in yourself to come through. You want to know that your capabilities are there—no matter what! This frees you to actualize your potential and to do so much more regularly.

GROWING THROUGH OTHERS

Finding and embracing positive examples set by others is another very effective form of simulation. You can gain greatly from attempting to replicate or live some of the positive attributes of a highly respected performer or person. You consciously set out to borrow the best attributes from another person or performer in an attempt to improve yourself. Sometimes when I see, meet, or get to know someone, I discover in that person something that I really like or admire. It could be a young child, a family member, or a great performer. It may be a physical, technical, psychological, or spiritual attribute. I think, *I'd like to move that way . . . to be open in that way . . . to handle problems like that . . .to express my feelings the way she does . . . to interact with the same ease . . . to use my time that way . . . to be relaxed like that . . . to carry myself that way. . . .to embrace my life in the same way, with the same passion. I really like the way he approaches performances, learns from everything . . . exudes confidence . . . hustles on the court. I like his relaxed style of paddling, her love for nature, his connection in play, the way he runs hills. I'm going to try it!*

You can look for and selectively draw upon other people's strengths in order to better yourself technically, physically, mentally, emotionally, or spiritually. You can literally attempt to be that person in certain respects, to see how it feels. You can see yourself as that great athlete in stance, in posture, in execution. You can tell yourself, *Today I'm going to pretend I'm so-and-so from the time I step out the door or onto the floor; I'm going to walk tall, the way he does, and try to execute my moves as gracefully; I'm going to be calm just like her, even if the coach starts yelling; I'm going to work really hard just like he does for the whole game.* You can make a conscious decision to be, or focus, a certain way for a specified period of time. If it feels right and helps you, hang on to it. If not, let it slide.

Some of the best professional impersonators and actors report that they can achieve things while impersonating or becoming others that they cannot achieve while being themselves. For example, they become funnier or more witty or reach a higher pitch in singing or experience a greater connection than in ordinary life. Embracing special qualities in others and within yourself is another path to becoming what you are capable of becoming. You might also see a behavior, a technique, or action, and say to yourself, *I am not going to be like that, perform like that, or act that way.* Then do everything possible to avoid behaving that way.

SUCCESS THROUGH SIMULATION: A CASE STUDY

Indonesian athletes were world champions in badminton for an unprecedented number of years. They had a history of winning when it counted. When they were the best in the world I watched them play; talked with them, their coaches, and their former world champions; and visited their training camps. One reason they were on top of the world so long was their extensive use of simulation training. They simulated every aspect of the game—for example, their strategy, coming from behind, bad calls, high temperature, crowd effects—particularly for the world championships.

STRATEGY

Long before the match, the top Indonesian players knew everything about their opponents—their strengths, weaknesses, playing style, and technical peculiarities. They studied videos of their opponents and gained from the experiences of teammates who had already faced them. They preplanned a strategy and mentally ran through exactly what they would do when their opponents did A, B, or C. Teammates sometimes role-played the actions of opponents in simulated games. They knew where they should return the bird for a particular opponent before they played him, and they prepared to place the bird accordingly before it ever reached them in the actual game.

They also practiced anticipating their opponents' returns, which meant knowing beforehand where the bird would likely go and planning to be there. If this strategy worked on 7 out of 10 shots, it was worth targeting the anticipated return area. In a sport like badminton, speed is closely linked to anticipation. The player must anticipate and move toward the return area before the bird is fully hit, particularly for a hard smash. (This situation is similar to a hockey goalie facing a slap shot. To be successful, he must anticipate where the puck will go and be there before the player makes full contact with the puck. The puck moves to the goal faster than a goalie's capacity to react; correct anticipation is therefore essential.) By studying where the bird usually goes under various conditions and with different opponents, a player could greatly increase the chances of being in the right place at the right time. There is no doubt that the top Indonesian players were quick, but they had much more than speed: they knew where and when to move. They were almost always in the return area before the bird arrived, even on blistering shots in doubles play. Their speed was well directed, their opponents' shots were well anticipated, and their own strategies were well practiced through simulation training.

COMING FROM BEHIND

Top players built confidence in their ability to come from behind and win a game by simulating such situations in practice. They may start a game at 14 to 3—a stronger player would begin with 3 or 4 points and a weaker player with 13 or 14 points. The objective for the stronger player was to come back and win the game. For the weaker player, the objective was to prevent this from happening, or at least to have some strong rallies. With a proper matchup, both players could play hard and the stronger player would come back to win. This process gave less experienced players a chance to play the champions and the champions practice coming from behind. For many years in the Thomas Cup championships, whenever the Indonesian players did fall behind, they were consistently able to come on strong to win. The fact that they were behind did not seem to distract them at all; they had practiced coming back. They knew they would come back and they did.

BAD CALLS

Poor officiating—for example, calling a shuttle out of bounds when it is obviously in bounds—was simulated in practice to prepare players to overcome the frustration that can follow a bad call. The purpose of simulation was discussed, and would then be implemented in some practice games as well as in exhibitions. Sometimes the simulating "official" would make a series of bad calls. The player's goal was to ignore bad calls and focus on preparing for the next shot, to shift focus from something beyond his control to something within his control. There were no emotional outbursts or even second looks from the Indonesian players after questionable or close calls at the championships. They simply got on with the game.

HIGH TEMPERATURE

For many years, the Thomas Cup championships were held in Jakarta under extreme temperature conditions. The outside air temperature in the evening was in the mid-30s Celsius (mid-90s Fahrenheit), and the humidity was in the 90s. The arena was packed with 12,000 sweaty people, and there was no air conditioning. In addition, there were heat-producing television lights right next to the court, and all windows and doors were closed to prevent the drift of the shuttles. Needless to say, it was hot! The spectators ended up dripping wet just sitting in the stands.

How did the Indonesian players prepare for these conditions? They prepared by living and playing in the heat and by bringing in large crowds to fill extremely hot and humid arenas for exhibition matches. If visiting teams are to play to capacity under such extreme temperature conditions, they must also prepare for them. The best preparation is to practice and play exhibition games for a couple of weeks in the same time zone, in a similar climate, under similar conditions, and then rest well before the tournament. This prepares an athlete to walk into that arena and feel totally prepared to go the distance.

CROWD EFFECTS

I never heard a crowd roar as loudly as the crowd in Jakarta for the badminton championships. It was deafening, and it was a very partisan crowd. They heckled opponents and roared approval for their heroes' every shot. (The fact that a lot of private betting was associated with these games may explain some of the fans' enthusiasm.) In some countries a crowd of 12,000 people for a badminton match is unheard of; in Indonesia it was normal. The audience would be even larger if the seating capacity in the halls were greater. Younger players learned to adapt to these crowds by growing up with them. The junior players and national team members traveled throughout the country giving exhibitions to large crowds. They invited the public to the main badminton hall in Jakarta for simulation matches in final preparation for the championships; the free invitation was accepted gratefully, and the hall was full. This final simulation was aimed at readying the athletes to walk onto the championship court feeling totally prepared mentally.

The best players often took on more in their training than was required for their championships. For example, they may play one and a half to two hours straight at a very fast pace. They may play whole games where one player is allowed only to lob, or smash, or play defensively, or play to the backhand, while the other player can use all his moves. To keep the pace moving, to work on speed, and to develop anticipation, one player may play against two opponents, or multishuttle games may be introduced. In multishuttle games it is possible to play nonstop badminton—with a shuttle always in play— or to practice reacting to shuttles coming rapid-fire from all corners of the court.

As a result of training for more than is actually required on the day of the competition, the players were in superb physical condition. They used their fitness to their advantage, particularly in extreme temperature conditions. They could maintain a very fast pace or deliberately keep a rally or game going a long time, simply to tire out their opponents.

TALLER PLAYERS

When the taller European players started to play very well at the international level, the Indonesians developed a new simulation strategy to train their players to play more effectively against taller players. They built courts that were higher on one side, so that the players playing on that side were the same height as the top taller European players.

A former world champion and one of badminton's all-time greats believed that following three simple rules, which could easily be applied in practice simulation, gave a player an advantage both strategically and psychologically:

1. Never stop a game to change a shuttle when you are winning. If you lose two points in a row, change the shuttle.
2. Continue to use serves and shots that are working—often—but also use variation in your play- otherwise at the higher levels your opponents will effectively anticipate your shots.
3. Never change a winning tactic or strategy.

It is interesting to note that while still at the top of their game, the Indonesian superstars worked directly with the most promising junior players. The reigning and longtime world champions in both singles and doubles spent about two days a week coaching and playing with younger players. The youthful players had an opportunity to play with their heroes, to watch them at close range, to learn from them, to follow their actions, and to be inspired by them. The championship players also gained from the exchange and enjoyed it very much.

If you want to become a champion, train with the best. If you are already a champion, let younger athletes train with you so that you can help them in their pursuit of excellence. The only country where I witnessed in-depth simulation training that equaled or surpassed that of Indonesia was in China. In table tennis, a sport that the Chinese dominated for many years, they used simulation extensively and in some very creative ways. In the early 1980s some of the high-quality simulation procedures used with their best table tennis players were also being applied in badminton. In the latter 1980s China became the dominant badminton power in the world, defeating Indonesia.

The Chinese are masters of the art of simulation. It has played a major role in their traditional martial arts (Wushu) for many years and more recently has been applied in many contemporary sports such as badminton, volleyball, gymnastics, and diving. With their most successful teams, the Chinese went a step beyond most other countries in the extent to which they repeated skills or programs in training. They prepared athletes to perform when fatigued and to be ready to play specific opponents. For example, some skilled Chinese athletes were trained to replicate the playing styles of opponents from other countries so they could provide simulation training for national team members. Such training strengthened athletes' overall readiness to face the challenges of high-level opponents—with one important stipulation. It was critical that adequate rest time be allowed and that individual differences be respected.

It is interesting to note that when other countries learned about and began to make extensive use of the effective simulation training strategies that were developed by the Indonesian badminton players, those countries became the world leaders in badminton (for example, China, Malaysia, Korea, Denmark, Sweden, and England).

Similarly, when the Europeans began to implement some of the extensive simulation preparation strategies used by the Chinese in table tennis, they became world leaders in that sport (for example, Sweden). The bottom line here is that simulation is a very effective training strategy for any performance domain.

Chapter 13

Enter the Zen Zone

One of the most intriguing aspects of sports and the arts as they were originally practiced in Asia long ago was their focus on training the mind. Zen was developed and experienced through the martial arts and the fine arts, but its ultimate purpose was for enhancing the living of life itself.

For me, the most important lesson of Zen is the concept of oneness, a concept that was also embraced by many of our aboriginal people, including North American Indians and the Inuit people (eskimos) who inhabited the Canadian Arctic. Entering the Zen zone means becoming one with and inseparable from the essence of what you are doing during each moment you are actually doing it. It is being all here, totally present, absorbing yourself in, connecting yourself to, and becoming one with your body, your task, nature, the tree

> Childlikeness has to be restored with long years of training in the art of self-forgetfulness. When this is attained, man does his great works. He thinks yet he does not think.
>
> **Daisetz T. Suzuki**

you are looking at, the child you are playing with, the person you are talking with. When you are totally engaged in the process of doing, in a sense you become what you are doing and suspend all judgments about yourself, others, or your performance. If you begin to reflect, deliberate, question, condemn, or judge along the way, you lose your pure connection or become disconnected, apart from, separate, tentative, distracted. The original natural childlike bond between mind and mind, mind and body, mind and task, mind and creation, or mind and nature is broken. There are times for thinking and reflection, but there are also times to connect totally with what you are doing and to leave your conscious thinking behind. Performance is a time for connection rather than reflection.

TRANSCENDING TECHNIQUE

I often wondered how the great fencing masters prepared for duels in the old days, before the time when touches were recorded on an electronic scoreboard. How did the great swordsmen prevent themselves from becoming too distracted by outcomes and suffering a fatal performance flaw when the stakes were literally life or death? Many overly anxious swordsmen did not live to tell their tales, but what of those who survived and continued to excel?

Daisetz T. Suzuki, in his excellent book *Zen and Japanese Culture* (Suzuki 1993) touches eloquently on this question. Suzuki discusses the connection between Zen and the ancient art of swordsmanship as follows:

> If one really wishes to be master of an art, technical knowledge is not enough. One has to transcend technique so that the art grows out of the unconscious. . . . You must let the unconscious come forward. In such cases, you cease to be your own conscious master but become an instrument in the hands of the unknown. The unknown has no ego-consciousness and consequently no thought of winning the contest. . . . It is for this reason that the sword moves where it ought to move and makes the contest end victoriously. This is the practical application of the Lao-tzuan doctrine of doing by not doing. (Suzuki 1993, 94, 96)

For a swordsman to excel or even survive, he had to free himself from all ideas of life and death, gain and loss, right and wrong, giving himself up to a power that lives deeply within him. In essence he had to clear his mind of all irrelevant thoughts, follow his trained instincts, and trust his body to lead. The swordsman who performed at the highest level of excellence was likened to a scarecrow that "is not endowed with a mind, but still scares the deer" (Suzuki 1959, 100).

Suzuki continued, "A mind unconscious of itself is a mind that is not at all disturbed by effects of any kind. . . . It fills the whole body, pervading every part of the body . . . flowing like a stream filling each corner." If it should find a resting place anywhere, it is a state of "no thinking," "emptiness," "no-mind-ness" or "the mind of no mind" (Suzuki 1993, 111).

▪ FREEING MIND AND BODY

All at once I forgot the public, the other bullfighters, myself, and even the bull; I began to fight as I had so often by myself at night in the corrals and pastures, as precisely as if I had been drawing a design on a blackboard. They say that my passes with the cape and my work with the muleta that afternoon were a revelation of the art of bullfighting. I don't know, and I'm not competent to judge. I simply fought as I believe one ought to fight, without a thought, outside of my own faith in what I was doing. With the last bull I succeeded for the first time in my life in delivering myself and my soul to the pure joy of fighting without being consciously aware of an audience.

Juan Belmonte, the great Spanish bullfighter, reflected on the moment when he first freed his body and mind to dance within a performance.

▪ REACTING NATURALLY

For me it was a feeling of separating my body from my conscious mind and letting my body do what came naturally. When this happened things always went surprisingly well, almost as if my mind would look at what my body was doing and say, *Hey, you're good.* But at the same time not making any judgments on what I was doing because it was not "me" that was doing it; it was my body. This way, by not making any judgments, it was easy to stay in the present.

Canadian Olympian Kim Alleston spoke of a similar phenomenon.

Professional figure skater Charlene Wong and Olympic downhill skier Kellie Casey became exceptionally good at drawing on the Zen perspective to free themselves in their quests for personal excellence. When Charlene "turned on her autopilot," a wonderful program unfolded. When Kellie suspended conscious thinking and "let her body lead," she had a great run. For the duration of their best performances, they both suspended critical evaluation and trusted the body-mind connection to work without interference from conscious thought.

In the ancient art of swordsmanship, focusing was intimately connected with life. In Suzuki's words, "When a stroke is missed, all is lost eternally; no idle thinking could enter here." A consciousness too occupied with irrelevant thoughts and feelings stands in the way of "successfully carrying out the momentous business of life and death, and the best way to cope with the situation is to clear the field of all useless rubbish and to turn the consciousness into an automaton in the hands of the unconscious" (Suzuki 1959, 117).

Distracting thoughts or emotions could result in a swordsman's failing to see or detect "the movements of the enemy's sword with the immediacy of the moon casting its reflection on the water" (Suzuki

© Bongarts Photography/SportsChrome USA

When you are totally engaged in the process of doing, in a sense you become what you are doing.

1993, 133). Seeing and instantaneous action of body and limbs are essential. This is no place for minds obscured by irrelevant thought or clouded by anxiety. No obstruction should come between mind and movement.

As one Japanese Zen master pointed out, you can read the environment much more clearly when you are "calm internally," just as you can see the reflection more clearly on a calm lake than on a disturbed one. Anxiety is like wind that disturbs the image on a calm lake.

Suzuki points out that the perfect swordsman takes no cognizance of the enemy's personality, no more than of his own. For he is an indifferent onlooker of the fatal drama of life and death in which he himself is the most active participant. The swordsman's unconscious is free from the notion of self. As soon as the mind "stops" with an object of whatever nature, you cease to be master of yourself and are sure to fall victim to the enemy's sword (Suzuki 1993, 96-97).

Suzuki goes on to say that an idea, no matter how worthy and desirable in itself, becomes a disease when the mind is obsessed with it. The obsessions the swordsman has to get rid of are

1. the desire for victory,
2. the desire to resort to technical cunning,
3. the desire to display all that he has learned,
4. the desire to overawe the enemy,
5. the desire to play a passive role, and
6. the obsession to get rid of whatever obsession he is likely to be infected with (Suzuki 1993, 153-154).

"When any one of these obsesses him, he becomes its slave, as it makes him lose all the freedom he is entitled to as a swordsman." Whenever and wherever the mind is obsessed with anything, "make haste to detach yourself from it" (Suzuki 1993, 154). The primary reason that these obsessions can interfere with pure performance or excellence is that they interfere with gaining the purest connection with your performance.

The following quotations from Yagyu Tajima, the great 16th-century Japanese swordsman, provide some Eastern visions to reflect upon (Suzuki 1993, 114-115):

- "Emptiness is one-mind-ness, one-mind-ness is no-mind-ness, and it is no-mind-ness that achieves wonders."

- "Give up thinking as though not giving it up. Observe the technique as though not observing."
- "Have nothing left in your mind, keep it thoroughly cleansed of its contents, and then the mirror will reflect the images in their 'isness.'"
- "Turn yourself into a doll made of wood: it has no ego, it thinks nothing; and let the body and limbs work themselves out in accordance with the discipline they have undergone. This is the way to win."

A fencer with whom I worked stimulated my thinking about performing without thinking and without thinking about not thinking. He combined some aspects of Eastern and Western approaches to improve his fencing performance. He developed a precompetition plan that helped him start in a calmer and more relaxed state. What he wanted most was to compete in a Zen mind-set. In the beginning he wrote out a list of quotations that triggered in him the primary feelings of a Zen perspective. They included the following:

1. Zen is against conceptualization. The experience is the thing. Verbalism often becomes an empty abstraction.
2. If you want to see, see right at once. When you think, you miss the point.
3. When I look at a tree, I perceive that one of the leaves is red, and my mind stops with this leaf. When this happens, I see just one leaf and fail to take cognizance of the innumerable other leaves of the tree. If instead of this I look at the tree without any preconceived ideas, I shall see all the leaves. One leaf effectively stops my mind from seeing all the rest. When the mind moves on without stopping, it takes up hundreds of leaves without fail.
4. To think that I am not going to think of you anymore is still thinking of you. Let me then try not to think that I am not going to think of you.
5. Do not rely on others, or on the readings of the masters. Be your own lamp.
6. You have mastered the art when the body and limbs perform by themselves what is assigned to them to do with no interference from the mind.

The fencer read these quotations to himself several times before competing, as a reminder of the state of mind that he sought. He had some initial success but also some subsequent difficulty in maintaining this approach throughout his most crucial bouts. He refined his approach into a series of key words (for example, *It, it . . . be with it* or *Be here . . . be all here*), which he plugged in whenever he experienced too many thoughts or too much anxiety. As he went out to compete he began to tell himself, *You're here to fence, and nothing beyond the experience of fencing really matters . . . just go out and fence and enjoy yourself.* When he was able to follow these simple reminders, his body took over and he moved in an incredibly fluid way—sometimes making touch after touch without thought. After bouts like this he occasionally found himself wondering where all those great moves came from.

The fencer could not always enter this state, but it began to happen more frequently with less thought and more tournaments. He began searching for competitions in order to practice improving his mindset and letting his performance flow. Improving his overall perspective toward competition was his primary goal, but he also found help in backup strategies such as verbal reminders and relaxation when he ran into problems. A Zen orientation is not something that can be accomplished hurriedly, but it is certainly responsive to nurturing, as the fencer's comments make clear.

■ For the first few competitions, after reading and talking and thinking, I realized that I was too focused on what was wrong in the bout. I paid attention to what was wrong. To turn that around, I got back into the doing. I went into one tournament thinking, *There's nothing that says I have to be tied up in a competition.* The first two bouts were great, then I started to tie up. I couldn't let go of the feeling. I was first able to turn it around by becoming interested in everything around me, instead of being too worried about the expectations of others. This took a bit of time. I had to be in the competition. With each subsequent competition I had better and better control for more and more of the time. The coach stayed away and let me work things out for myself. Telling me technical things at the last minute, or after I'd blown something, just made things worse. I thanked him for staying quiet.

When speaking about his last competition, the fencer said:

■ As I stepped up for the bout, I thought, *I am here for the fencing . . . nothing else matters . . . get into the experience.* At no time did the thought of winning or losing enter the picture. I got into the finals, which was my goal, and we won the team competition. The "pressure situation" didn't faze me. On one occasion one guy did upset me emotionally. I went into the corner, did some relaxation, read my Zen reminders, came back, and won a key match 5 to 0. My primary strategy worked fine and I gave myself reminders in the bout if I felt I needed them (for example, *I'm here to experience it*). Many people commented on how relaxed I was. I really enjoyed myself and beat four very good fencers. I was there to fence—that's all.

He ended our discussion by saying, "The event is the focus. If I focus on the event, the feeling comes automatically. So I just let my interest get absorbed in the event. I relax and enjoy it. Lots of hits are unintentional. The guy just runs into my point."

Certain things cannot be forced. You must free yourself to let them happen. You don't have to try to be happy. You simply live and experience the simple joys of life, and happiness comes as a by-product. In a similar vein, you don't have to consciously try to win in order to win. During the contest you simply get absorbed in the experience; be in the present, trust your body, allow the performance program that has been ingrained in your mind and body to unfold, and the winning takes care of itself.

CHAPTER 14

SELF-HYPNOSIS

One way to turn more of our life dreams into reality is through self-hypnosis, a state of relaxed receptivity that can release some of the untapped potential within each of us. My father, Dr. Emanuel Orlick, has worked in the area of hypnosis and self-directed mind control for over 70 years. At age 90 he is still living on a farm and writing a regular column for the *Journal of Hypnosis.* I am thankful that he consented to share his perspectives on hypnosis by writing this chapter.

BELIEF IS THE MOTHER OF REALITY.

EXCELLENCE IS A STATE OF MIND.

THE POWER WITHIN

Humans everywhere are looking inside as well as outside themselves, seeking to develop or utilize talents, abilities, or powers that they feel they possess. No matter how excellent you are, you can be better. This is true for all of your mind-body attributes, talents, and abilities. No matter how good any of these may be now, they can be better—much better.

All of us have within us amazing mind-body powers that are sometimes brought into play when we face life-or-death situations. Almost every newspaper has on file eyewitness accounts of people who have performed incredible feats of strength in dire emergencies. For example, all of the major news media carried reports of a 110-pound mother who lifted the back of a station wagon off the crushed legs of her screaming 17-year-old son after a jack slipped and he was trapped beneath.

We all live and function far below our maximum mental and physical limits until something of sufficient importance triggers the use of our dormant mental and physical powers. Somehow, self-hypnosis can act as this triggering mechanism, thus enabling ordinary humans to perform superhuman mental and physical feats. With practice, each of us can boost our normal, everyday mind-body levels much higher than they are now.

Vasili Alexeev, one of the all-time greatest Russian weightlifters, was able to tap into his own mind-body potential. Before each lift he appeared to enter a trancelike hypnotic state. You could feel his intense concentration penetrate your own mind as he stood over the ponderous barbell at his feet, preparing himself mentally to thrust it over his head. You had the feeling that it was not only muscle power but some form of psychic energy that enabled Alexeev to lift those enormous poundages and break one record after another.

Self-hypnosis substitutes one powerful, positive, dominating thought for a number of distracting, competing, negative thoughts; it substitutes one powerful, positive belief for a number of competing negative beliefs; it substitutes one powerful *I can* for a number of competing *I can'ts*; it suspends a host of "normal" critical, doubting, restraining, interfering thoughts and focuses all of the relevant mind-body faculties on the accomplishment of one goal to the exclusion of all competing goals. Perhaps the simplest way to describe the focusing aspect of hypnosis is to compare it to a magnifying glass that can concentrate ordinary, harmless sun rays so strongly into one narrow point that they burn a hole through a piece of paper.

ENHANCING PERFORMANCE

Self-hypnosis and autosuggestion have the capacity to enhance your performance. In *self-hypnosis* you put yourself into a relaxed, receptive state. In this state the normal critical faculties of conscious mind are temporarily suspended. Thus, you become receptive to any strong or repetitive suggestions you make to yourself, either directly or indirectly. Under self-hypnosis you may talk to yourself, read previously prepared scripts, listen to prerecorded scripts, or listen to scripts being read by another person. In self-hypnosis you control everything, from start to finish, in each session.

In *autosuggestion* you directly or indirectly influence your own thoughts or actions in the conscious, waking state. Autosuggestion can be intentional or unintentional and may have positive or negative effects. An example of positive autosuggestion can be seen in Muhammad Ali's constant repetition of the phrase, "I am the greatest." His use of this phrase and his subconscious belief in himself played a major role in his rise to become one of the greatest boxers ever and in the length of time he stayed at the top.

Both positive autosuggestion and self-hypnosis can help you in your performance activities. You can use autosuggestion by reading short scripts over and over again; by repeating positive phrases to yourself; and by playing recorded suggestions to yourself as you drive to school, work, or training, or at any other time.

Think of your brain as a highly sophisticated computer that you program to direct your body in a certain way, as the space center computers direct an unmanned vehicle to land on Mars. Your body is the vehicle, your brain is the computer. Once the brain is programmed, your body must follow its commands, must seek out the goals you have established, and must strive constantly to achieve them. You are the programmer, and you determine what you will feed into your brain.

Think of your ultimate goal. This goal must be etched into your neuron pattern so deeply and so strongly that you will do everything in your power to achieve it. You must believe, with every fiber of your being, not only that you can achieve it and must achieve it, but also that you will achieve it. I have never met a person who was a success at anything who did not believe in his or her ability to succeed. Unfortunately, most of the people around us, including our own families and coaches, spend more time telling us what we cannot do than what we can do. Therefore, your first step is to instill in yourself an unshakable belief.

Through self-hypnosis your normal critical, judgmental, or negative thinking can be suspended temporarily, so that the highest possible degree of absolute belief can be inculcated more rapidly. Once the belief becomes a permanent part of your subconscious thought process, you will automatically behave in accordance with this belief.

SIMPLE STEPS TO SELF-HYPNOSIS

The secret of self-hypnosis is twofold:

1. You must fixate your conscious attention.
2. You must relax your body.

The moment you do these two things, you are actually in self-hypnosis. Pick a spot on the wall in front of you right now and stare at it while you let your body become limp and relaxed. Keep staring and relaxing for a few moments, and you will feel yourself sinking deeper and deeper into self-hypnosis.

Self-hypnosis in sport can help you believe in yourself and reach your potential.

That is all there is to it. Even in this very light hypnotic state, you can begin to program yourself with beneficial positive suggestions. Anyone can put himself into self-hypnosis simply by fixating his conscious attention and relaxing. With practice, you can go deeper and deeper and the programming will become more and more effective. Even in the lightest state of hypnosis you can accomplish remarkable things, such as eliminating the pain of a throbbing headache, curing insomnia, improving your concentration, and so on.

The remainder of this chapter is aimed at helping you fixate your conscious attention, relax your body, and make your subconscious mind more and more receptive to the beneficial positive suggestions that you will make to yourself. Once you are in a relaxed, receptive state, the most important thing is repetition. Whether you are programming yourself for the first time, reprogramming yourself, or reinforcing past programming, it is important that you repeat each positive suggestion many times to implant it deeply and firmly in your subconscious mind.

FOUR STEPS TO FOLLOW

Effective self-hypnosis involves fixation, relaxation, receptivity, and repetitive suggestion.

FIXATION

It really doesn't matter on what external object you fixate your conscious attention. However, one of the most effective objects is either a candle or a black dot in the middle of a piece of white paper. Any piece of white paper will do, and the black dot can be any size you wish. I usually use an index card on which I draw a circle with the help of a dime and then fill in the circle with a black marking pen. This gives me a focus point on which to concentrate my attention. I have found that I get the best results when this card is placed about 12 inches (31 centimeters) away from my eyes and a little above them. Also, I prefer to face a blank wall, preferably dark, with the light coming from somewhere behind me.

RELAXATION

Over the years I have developed my own method of relaxation, which I believe is most effective for use in hypnosis. I call it the *think into* method because you must think into your various body parts to make it work. You may have some difficulty thinking into some body parts the first time you try it, but after a few attempts it will be extremely easy.

To facilitate relaxation when you are about to induce self-hypnosis, it is helpful to follow a specific sequence—for example, starting with your toes, working your way up your body, and ending with your fingers. After a few practice sessions you will be able to do the whole procedure from memory, without referring to the instructions that follow. At first it will take a few minutes as you read and think into the body parts listed, but before long you will do it in a matter of seconds.

The sequence is as follows:

1. Think into your toes. Let your mind scan your toes like an X-ray machine. With your mind, command your toes to *relax, relax, relax.*

2. Think into your feet. Let your mind scan your feet like an X-ray machine. With your mind, command your feet to *relax, relax, relax.*

3. Think into your calves. Let your mind scan your calves like an X-ray machine. With your mind, command your calves to *relax, relax, relax.*

Repeat exactly the same think-into sequence for your thighs, buttocks, abdomen, lower back, chest, upper back, shoulders, neck, face, arms, hands, and fingers.

After you have followed these instructions three or four times, close your eyes and do the sequence from memory. Start with your toes and work up your body as described, and finish with your fingers. It is not necessary to think into every body part I mentioned. The important thing is to reach the major segments of your body and the muscle groups that activate them.

RECEPTIVITY

Fixation and deep relaxation lead to a state of receptivity for positive suggestion. With practice you will be able to enter this state more completely and more quickly, until the time comes when you will be able to relax instantly just by saying to yourself, *relax, relax, relax.* Not only will this increase your receptivity to self-hypnosis, but it will help you eliminate undesirable stress and tension whenever the need arises.

REPETITIVE SUGGESTION

To develop the greatest possible control over your body and yourself, prepare a short script to read, to think to yourself, or to play back on tape a number of times when you have put yourself into the relaxed, receptive hypnotic state. Your self-suggestions can relate to any area in which you would like to improve. Your script should be short, powerful, and positive. Repeat the script three times. The most effective procedure is to first use repetitive self-suggestions during self-hypnosis and to follow this up with autosuggestion during the event itself. Following are three sample scripts, with pointers for their use.

Sample 1. My tremendously powerful brain has absolute control over all of the cells, tissues, and organs that make up my entire body. It has complete control over all of my feelings, emotions, and reactions. If I feel the jitters coming on, I will simply say to myself, *relax, relax,* and the jitters will vanish.

Repeat this script to yourself a number of times during each self-hypnosis session until it becomes implanted deeply and firmly in your subconscious mind. Then, whenever you do feel the jitters coming on and want to control them, just repeat the words *relax, relax,* and they will vanish.

Sample 2. I am an outstanding player. I have everything it takes to achieve my goals. I will remain focused in the present. Whenever I shoot I will focus directly on the open space and shoot directly into that space. I will shoot and score. I will shoot and score. I will shoot and score.

When sitting on the bench, during a practice or a game, you can reinforce the script through autosuggestion. Repeat to yourself, *I am a skilled player, I have everything I need to achieve my goals. I will think and look and shoot at the best open space. I will score goals. I will stay focused on the step in front of me.*

Sample 3. I love running. I am in great physical condition and I am improving every day. I have a very powerful brain and body. When I run, my brain and body combine their power to speed up the flow of oxygen and nutrients to my hard-working muscles. They work in complete harmony to speed up the removal of waste products from my muscles. I am strong and efficient.

While running, visualize the oxygen and nutrients flowing to your working muscles and the waste products being removed from your working muscles. While running, also repeat the words *relax, relax* to yourself, thinking into your arms and legs and other working body parts. This will encourage better relaxation between the vigorous contractions and speed up recovery between each thrust, thereby helping you increase your running efficiency. As you begin to feel your body extending itself, say over and over to yourself, *Strong and efficient . . . strong and efficient . . . I could run forever.*

Whatever you want to accomplish, you must think it, see it, feel it, and do it. The evening before you enter any event, no matter how unimportant it may be, you can choose to use self-hypnosis to do your very best. Think to yourself, *I will perform my best; I will perform to my capacity.* Imagine yourself doing your best and finishing the way you want to finish.

On the day of the event, for which you have prepared properly, think and say to yourself over and over again, *I feel great! I feel terrific! Today I am going to perform my best!* As you repeat these positive thoughts to yourself, make yourself feel great, and really do your utmost to perform the best race you have ever run. Think it. See it. Feel it. Believe it and do it.

GETTING STARTED

You now have the information you need to put yourself in self-hypnosis and to begin to use this power to draw out and develop your mental and physical capabilities.

Select a quiet room where you can complete your entire self-hypnosis session without being disturbed.

Place your focus object—a candle or a white card with a black dot—in front of the place where you will sit, making sure that it is about 12 inches (31 centimeters) away from your eyes and a little above them.

Place your scripts or other self-programming materials (for example, tapes and tape player) on a table just in front of your chair. If you have memorized your script or know exactly what you want to program into yourself, so much the better. Sit down on a fairly comfortable chair facing your focus point. Get yourself into a receptive state.

Place your forearms on the table with the palms of your hands facing down.

Think relaxation. Think of every muscle in your entire body becoming soft and limp.

Stare at the focus object. Take a fairly deep breath, hold it for a moment, and then let it out slowly. As you exhale, say to yourself, *relax, relax, relax.* Repeat this breathing and exhaling process seven times, letting your entire body become more limp and more relaxed each time.

Your eyes will begin to water. Then they will blink and your eyelids will get heavier and heavier until it is all you can do to keep them open. The moment your eyes begin to blink, or water, or close, you will know that you are sinking into the receptive state of self-hypnosis. A tingling sensation in your hands or fingers is another indication. Don't worry about being sure you are under or how deep you are under. If you follow the steps outlined here, you will be receptive to your own positive self-suggestions.

If you want to sink still deeper, then say to yourself, *I am sinking, sinking, sinking, deeper, deeper, and deeper.* Repeat this a number of times and then say to yourself, *I am now in a deep, deep, deep state of self-hypnosis, and I am sinking deeper and deeper and deeper.* You must see yourself sinking deeper and deeper; you must feel yourself sinking deeper and deeper; you must really believe that you are sinking deeper and deeper; and you will sink deeper and deeper.

After taking your seven fairly deep breaths, start your thinking-into sequence, beginning with your toes and ending up with your fingers as described earlier. Do this mentally with your eyes closed; command each body part, as you scan it with your mind, to *relax, relax, relax.*

By the time you reach your fingers, you should be in a very relaxed, self-hypnotized, receptive state, and you may proceed to feed any desired suggestions directly into your powerful subconscious mind. Do this by opening your eyes and reading your prepared script. Before doing so, be sure to tell yourself that you will remain in the relaxed, receptive hypnotic state even after you open your eyes. If you have taped your script, you may open your eyes, switch on your tape player, and then close your eyes again. Or you can have a close, trusted friend or teammate turn on your tape or read the script to you when you are in the hypnotic state. If you are alone without a tape, it may be best to first memorize your script and to then simply repeat the suggestions to yourself as you fall into the hypnotic state.

At the completion of each self-hypnosis session, while you are still in the very relaxed, receptive state, say to yourself, *When I hold my next self-hypnosis session, I will be able to enter a deep state of self-hypnosis quickly and easily.*

Finally, just before you are ready to wake up, say to yourself, *When I count three I will wake up, and when I wake up I will feel great, I will feel terrific, I will feel better than I have ever felt before.* Then count *one, two, three,* and wake up feeling rejuvenated.

If you go to bed immediately after your self-hypnosis session, sleep will come rapidly and the powerful suggestions that you have just given yourself will become even more deeply entrenched in your subconscious mind.

When you awake next morning, say to yourself, *I feel great—I feel terrific*—and you really will. Think it! Believe it! And act accordingly.

For more detailed information on self-hypnosis for sport, or for specific self-programming scripts developed by Emanuel Orlick, see the references and resources section (page 235).

Chapter 15

Making Your Strategies Work for You

You now have at your disposal some of the major means to positive mental control and excellence. If you experiment with some of these approaches, your options for personal growth will become clearer and your pursuit more successful. But you must act upon knowledge for it to be of real value. You must experience strategies to understand them and to discover how they can be most helpful for you. This means practicing an approach or coping strategy long enough, and often enough, for its positive effects to surface in a consistent and natural way. Even when no visible signs of improvement are immediately evident, you are often laying the foundation for future personal growth.

> Man cannot discover new oceans unless he has courage to lose sight of the shore.
>
> **André Gide**

PERSISTENCE

A big part of the challenge of pursuing excellence is to be persistent in pursuing your goals and to continue to accept yourself throughout the ongoing growth process. When you apply specific self-growth strategies to your personal situation, expect improvement, but don't expect instant miracles. For example, if you've been highly anxious in competitive situations for years, don't be disappointed and give up on a strategy if you are not totally calm by tomorrow. Although I have witnessed dramatic—literally overnight—improvements, self-growth is more often a progression. Take it step by step, day by day, moment by moment, and be persistent. You will have ups and downs in mental training just as you do in physical training. Sometimes you will feel mentally strong and totally in control; other times you may temporarily slide back into less constructive ways of thinking and thereby upset yourself or underestimate your potential. But you will roll back into control. With persistence you will become fully focused and in control more and more of the time.

I deliberately use the term *persistence* rather than *effort*. With some approaches, persistence involves noneffort rather than effort. Did you ever try to go to sleep and end up tossing and turning for what seems like hours? You keep telling yourself, *I have to get to sleep; try to go to sleep.* Then as soon as you stop trying so hard, you slip away effortlessly into slumber. In some cases, noneffort, or less conscious effort, yields results that forced effort continually chases away. You can achieve some things more readily by "trying easier," by taking your time, or moving toward your goal in an unhurried way.

Persistence means giving something enough time to work. Don't be too quick to say, "I tried that and it didn't work." How long did you try it? How often did you practice it? How fully did you focus on it? Did you gradually introduce the strategy, first in a relaxed setting and then under more stressful circumstances? Did you provide yourself with enough opportunities to allow the feeling, or focus, to surface naturally without rushing for instant results?

Often when a self-growth strategy does not work, it is because of a lack of full focus when implementing it or persistence in its application. For example, trying to refocus for one minute and saying it doesn't work is like training for a competition for one minute and claiming that it doesn't work. The one minute may not work, but more extensive, high-quality training does. The fact that an attempt doesn't work immediately is no indication that it will never work. Imagine if you had approached the refinement of physical skills in that way! How skilled would you be today?

It is true that some strategies will not be compatible with you, and you should not waste time on them. But if you do select a strategy that feels right—even a little bit right—give it a chance to work for you.

Remember these points when first introducing a new approach for self-growth or mental control:

- Go with what seems workable for you.
- Don't overload yourself with strategies; start with one or two.
- Try the approach in less stressful situations until you sort things out.
- Create a reminder to help bring on the desired response or focus (for example, *focus, power, flow, control, relax).*
- Practice using your reminder as a way into your best focus state.
- Before the day or event begins, think of the way you would like to feel that day or focus in that event; remind yourself of the perspective you want to carry.
- Let those positive feelings and connected focus surface naturally.
- Prepare a backup strategy in case the feeling or focus doesn't surface.
- Give your chosen strategy or strategies a chance to work.
- Expect improvement, but not overnight miracles.
- Be willing to lose a little in the short run to gain a lot in the long run.
- Remember that joy, experimentation, and persistent refinement are necessary for progress and perfection.

When you are trying new approaches or strategies, before they are well practiced, guard against thinking too much about what you are thinking about. A female fencer commented:

In the first two bouts of the tournament I was thinking so much about what I was thinking that I didn't fence. It took losses in those two bouts for me to realize what was happening. I was expecting everything to just happen and it didn't. Once I started to concentrate on fencing my opponent, things slowed down, I began to relax, and I won the next two bouts. The latter two wins were against much stronger fencers than the first two losses.

During the event, focus on the doing. A cat pursuing a mouse is not thinking about what she should be thinking about. She is focused on the doing. The purpose of your strategy is to get into that fully focused frame.

The best time to evaluate or to think about what you have thought about is after the event, unless an immediate change in focus is required within the match. In this case, do a brief evaluation and refocus at some break in the action—for example in fencing after the touch, point, or match. If thinking begins to interfere with your focus during the event, change channels by focusing on something constructive and concrete that will get you back on track.

The process of learning to connect fully, refine your focus, and channel your emotions in positive directions is a bit like learning to walk. You may wobble or even fall a number of times before you

During an event, focus on the doing.

become fully stable, balanced, and in control. You need the same kind of persistence to walk and run with your mental skills as you do for your physical skills.

Setting daily goals can help you become more persistent, as might writing yourself reminders and rewarding yourself for positive steps along the way. However, for any of these techniques to really work, you must really want to improve your focus, your performance, or your life. Everything begins with your commitment. No one can force you to want to grow or improve; this is a decision that must come from within yourself. Once you have made the decision, persistence does not guarantee that you will achieve your ultimate goals; it does guarantee that you will learn and grow along the way. Embracing a journey gives your life meaning—even when you do not arrive at a distant destination.

RETENTION OF PURPOSE

Chris Hadfield, a nine year-old Canadian farm boy, watched the first man walk on the moon via live television broadcast. From that moment on he wanted to be an astronaut. That vision drove every major decision he made for the rest of his life. At the time it was an impossible dream; there wasn't even an astronaut program in Canada. Still, he persisted while many other youngsters' dreams faded away. I asked Chris how he was able to persist through the many challenges and seemingly insurmountable obstacles he faced along the way. His response was simple—retention of purpose.

> If you want to achieve a very challenging goal, you have to have a reason for doing it, you have to really want to do it, you have to persist through a series of obstacles, you have to keep in mind why you are doing this and why it is important in your life. This retention of purpose or passion is what keeps you going towards your goal. There will be seemingly insurmountable setbacks if you set yourself any sort of difficult goal. You'll get to a stage where the whole horizon is black and you don't see any way through. That happened to me several times; I mean I chose as a kid to be an astronaut when I grew up. It was a black horizon from the beginning; there was no way; it was impossible at the time. But things always change, given time. There are always new possibilities.

The important part in achieving, or even coming close to what you dream of doing, is a retention of purpose. Every day you're going to have a choice to go a little bit closer to where you want to get, every single day. And then there will be some break points in your life where you really fundamentally choose whether you're going to head that direction or not. And if you don't make that choice, if you don't change direction you will end up where you're headed. Guaranteed. So you need to fundamentally choose which direction you want to go and start headed that way and maybe you'll get to where you want to go.

The purpose that I chose for myself, the goal I wanted to achieve as an adult, I internalized deliberately at nine years old. I was by no means a robot headed that way, but I always had choices and I thought, *Well, someday, maybe, I'll get to be an astronaut, and if I am, I really should know about this; I better study this; I should do this.* I was lucky enough that when I got to the point in my life where I was qualified, the opportunity arose and I was in a position to take advantage of it. I think that basic retention of purpose through a whole life, not only maybe gets you to your goal but also makes life more interesting and fulfilling because you're headed some direction that you like. And your life loses its random and therefore unfulfilling nature. I really enjoy it.

PART IV

LIVING
EXCELLENCE

CHAPTER 16

PREVENTING PANIC SITUATIONS

Preparing to excel in a performance domain is like preparing to climb a mountain or run a wilderness river. You must first embrace the challenge, plan an appropriate course, take stock of the difficulties, and find a way through the obstacles. When you choose a particular course, you do so for good reasons—and have a plan to get back on course if the current pulls you off course. You know this even before you start out. If you must change course in midstream because of some unforeseen obstacle, opportunity, or opening, you can be alert and adaptable enough to do so. If one approach does not work, you try another. In case you should capsize, you have a recovery plan so that all is not lost. The price of no backup plan on a wild river or challenging pursuit may be spinning out of control or plunging over a cliff or falls.

PERSONAL EXCELLENCE IS POSSIBLE ONLY IF YOU HAVE A DREAM AND A PLAN AND IF YOU PERSIST IN THE FACE OF ALL OBSTACLES.

To avoid potential problems in your pursuit, heed these reminders:

1. Embrace a challenge that you feel is worthy of you and your focus.
2. Plan a course that you feel can take you to your goals.
3. Run your course or game plan through your mind so you are clear about what you want to do.
4. Look the obstacles over; become familiar with them.
5. Plan a strategy to overcome them and a backup strategy, in case a problem arises.
6. Get onto your course, and remain alert and ready, mind wide open and body flowing.
7. Perceive the obstacles, but don't let your mind remain with them or you will be unprepared for the next step, challenge, or opportunity.
8. Continue to move forward, taking advantage of your strengths, opportunities, obstacles, and the flow of things around you.

If you begin to implement solutions before problems get out of hand, you will experience less distress and better results. This is like taking steps to prevent a headache from cropping up or introducing a remedy at the slightest sign of onset, instead of waiting until your head is pounding out of your skull; or feeding a baby at the first sign of hunger, not waiting until the infant is in a screaming rage. Ideally you anticipate and prepare to solve potential problems before they arise.

If you wait until a situation is totally out of control, or until you are in a panic mode, it becomes much more difficult to implement an effective solution. However, if you catch things early, or as they are surfacing *(Hey, cool it, relax, focus, listen, learn, act)*, you have a much better chance of regaining control quickly and staying in control.

So when you know that you will be entering a situation that has challenged you or created stress in the past, prepare yourself mentally and physically (for example, plan your path, have a walk or run, or do something that relaxes you) so that you begin in a calmer state. Even if your stress level does begin to rise as the challenge approaches—and it probably will—you will end up in a calmer and more focused state because you started in a calmer state.

PLANNING YOUR PSYCHOLOGICAL PATH

Performing your best when it counts most requires that you focus on doing what is ultimately best for you and your mission. Maintaining your best focus is easier to do if you bring a positive attitude into the situation, focus fully within the performance, and have a prepracticed plan for overcoming obstacles. You have to know what you want to do and how you are going to do it—before you do it. You need to know that you are going to carry a positive mind-set and an effective focus. You also need to know what you are going to do if something pulls you out of your best focus.

To be as prepared as possible, and to experience as few setbacks as possible, top performers develop an effective on-site focus plan and a personal refocusing plan.

An on-site focus plan usually includes your preferred preperformance and performance focus. It also outlines the sequence of events you will go through from the time you arrive at the performance site to the time you finish your performance. Your refocusing plan lists potential problems or distractions that could arise and your proposed means of avoiding, minimizing, or coping with each.

© Eric Sanford/International Stock

Having a plan for performance keeps you on the right path.

COMPLETING YOUR FOCUS PLAN

Four questions should be thought out, planned, and practiced before the event:

1. How do I want to focus ?
2. What should I do to get into that focus?
3. Why should I do it?
4. What should I do if it doesn't work?

A fifth question—*How did it go?*—lets you assess your effectiveness in implementing your plan and should be answered after the event.

HOW DO I WANT TO FOCUS?

What is my best performance focus for this event? How do I want to feel going into this event? How do I want to focus within my performance? WHAT should I do to get into that focus? What will help me enter my preferred focus?
Think about what you would like to do from the time you arrive at the performance site to the time you start your event—in order to feel the way you want, physically and mentally. List your preferred preparation activities in the actual sequence in which you would like them to occur. Use the following sample on-site focus plan (table 16.1) as a guide if you think it might help. Some performers prefer, and gain, from very detailed descriptions of activities, focus reminders, and actions. Others prefer more of a sketch to remind them of their best focus, while some simply recall the perspective they want to carry and let it unfold in the performance. Whatever approach you intend to follow, it should be planned and practiced. Ideally your game plan and on-site focus will be automatic (or almost automatic) by the time you implement it in an important event.

WHY SHOULD I DO IT?

After you have outlined your basic activities, procedures, and strategies, think about why you are following each of them. What do you expect to get from each in terms of your feelings, focus, or performance?

WHAT SHOULD I DO IF IT DOESN'T WORK?

Suppose that a procedure or strategy does not work the way you would like it to, or that it does not work at all. Then what are you

SAMPLE ON-SITE FOCUS PLAN
Event: Track Sprint

What is my best focus? Focus on the doing—one step at a time.

What should I do?	Why should I do it?	What should I do if it does not work?
General warm-up: long, slow stretching	To feel loose, relaxed, and calm	More stretching, *relax*, reminder—can run well no matter how warm-up feels
Event preparation: keep warm, active, stretch periodically until event time	To stay loose	Extra sweatsuit, run loose, relax
Replicate part of race at full speed, short duration but intense enough to sweat	To feel confident in speed	Visualize best previous race—feel it; then simulate first 20 meters
Simulate start with heat before with cue words	To feel ready for explosive start	Simulate in imagery if not possible physically—think *explosive* in imagery
See yourself, feel yourself run the way you want to run	As a last-minute reminder before letting body do it	Remind yourself how you want to feel and run
Approach blocks: *breathe, relax, ready, alert, strong*	To feel 100 percent ready	Remind self of past best, of untapped potential—*I need to feel butterflies; I'm going to run well*
In blocks: ready position, *breathe out, relax*	To feel everything's under control	Let shoulders relax, focus on breathing
Set position, think *blast off, blast off*	To fly off the blocks, hard to hold back, fast as lightning	*Explode, uncoil; spring like a cat*

1. How did it go?
2. Any changes required in plan for next time?

going to do? Think about it and find a backup strategy. Backup strategies are called into play only if the original strategy is not doing the job effectively. For the most part, backups will remain in reserve; but it is important to know that you can call on them if you need them.

How did it go?

When the performance or event is over, assess the overall effectiveness of your plan. How did it go? Preperformance? During the performance? What parts went well? What areas need additional work for improvement? Are any changes required in your focus plan, procedures, or strategies for next time?

Performers in all disciplines can gain from personalized, on-site focus plans. Every world champion, Olympic champion, and professional champion I have worked with or interviewed (and they have been numerous) has developed an effective way of mentally preparing for competition and knows how to focus consistently in a way that he or she has found effective. It is likely that you also have the beginnings of a plan that probably only needs refinement to take you where you want to go.

It is interesting that many athletes who experience their best performances in high-intensity events engage themselves in preplanned activities right up until the last few minutes before the performance. At that point there is a zoning in, a brief mental review of their best performance focus, and a complete connection with their task from the *start* signal to the end of their event.

If you think you might benefit from seeing the detailed focus plans of many great performers in various pursuits, see my books *Psyching for Sport: Mental Training for Athletes, Embracing Your Potential: Steps to Self-Discovery, Balance, and Success in Sports, Work, and Life,* and *Psyched: Inner Views of Winning* (see page 235).

MAKING YOUR REFOCUSING PLAN

At the World Student Games, track athletes were corralled in a cramped holding area for about 30 minutes before being lined up and marched directly from the entrance tunnel to the starting blocks. Their last possible contact with their coaches or teammates was more than 30 minutes before the event. At the Moscow Spartakiade, divers were crowded into an extremely small and impersonal waiting area between dives, giving some athletes a feeling of no personal space. As divers on the 10-meter platform prepared for their dives, large flags, strategically placed at eye level, began to move at the other end of the pool. At major competitions it is not uncommon to face 10 to 15 distractions in the course of one day.

Every performer can gain from having an effective refocusing plan for potential distractions. To develop your refocusing plan, start by listing the things that usually bother you at competitions, followed by other things that could bother you. Let's say you are preparing for a very important event that comes along only once or twice in a lifetime. You want to be as prepared as possible to cope with both expected and unexpected circumstances that you may face at this event. Therefore, find out as much as you can about what these events have been like for other performers or athletes in the past; you can learn from former competitors, athletes, coaches, videos, and articles. On the basis of your own experiences as well as the experiences of others, make an intelligent guess about what the event will be like for you and how you need to prepare for it.

Think about distractions or hassles that have affected you in the past, as well as particular things that are likely to happen at your upcoming event. Include distractions that could arise in the week or two leading up to the event; travelling; at the residence and training site; at the competition site; on the day of the event; within the performance; between halves, periods, or performances and after the competition. Develop a refocusing plan for what you feel might pose potential problems. Your aim is to avoid as many bothersome distractions as possible and to cope effectively with those that you cannot or do not wish to avoid. You may prefer that no storms blow your way; but if they should come, know how to avoid them and be well prepared to overcome them.

You can break your plan into major *if-then* components:

- *If* this happens, *then* I do this.
- *If* this doesn't work, *then* I do that.

Plan your strategy in detail. Write down reminders that will help you do what you want to do. Use your reminders in practices and simulated conditions. Become familiar enough with them to call upon them naturally in challenging situations.

If you have practiced "cooling it," relaxing your pace, changing channels, channeling your focus, accepting uncertainties, and embracing challenges, you are less likely to get upset over various kinds of distractions, changes in schedules, long waits, outside pressures, unfamiliar conditions, regimented procedures, or demanding expectations.

Unexpected things will often occur at important events. Although you cannot anticipate every possible adversity, you can prepare an effective on-site coping response to use in the face of almost all unexpected happenings. If you feel yourself starting to react negatively to something, use these distracting thoughts or negative feelings as a signal to *shift focus*. If you repeat *shift focus* several times in a row, it will generally break you away from the distracting thoughts long enough to refocus on something more constructive.

The whole coping sequence might unfold as follows: *I don't like these feelings and I don't have to stay with them. Shift focus—shift focus— shift focus. This doesn't have to bother me! It's no big deal. I can still do what I want to do. Relax. Focus!*

At this point you should focus fully on doing the skill you are doing, preparing to do the skill you are about to do, or something else that is immediate, absorbing, and constructive. If the distraction happens just before your performance, shift focus to your final preparations for executing your performance, the feel of it, the form of it, the flow of it, or the game plan you are going to follow. For example, take a deep breath, relax as you exhale, imagine what you want to do, then do it with full focus.

Focus your energy on things you can control rather than things you cannot control. We cannot control other people's thoughts or actions, the caliber of competition, or the past. We can, however, control our own preparation and our own performance. We can make every effort to focus in a way that will free us to do our personal best. No one can ask for more than that; no one can do more than that. Nothing beyond your sincere attempt to do your best really matters. Other competitors are other competitors and you are you, a totally separate entity. If you begin to compare yourself with others, use that as a reminder to focus on your own preparation, your own strategy, your own performance.

Your on-site focus plan and your refocusing plan allow you to enter performance situations with additional confidence. You have a well-thought-out and prepracticed plan to make things go right and a plan to use in case something goes wrong. You are ready.

CHAPTER 17

GETTING THE BEST FROM COACHES

Many coaches work extremely hard, have very good intentions, and do a great job, but some do not think enough about what is best for the unique individuals they are coaching. They may focus too much on results without giving adequate thought to you as a thinking, feeling human being. The best coaches understand that when you feel valued and respected, you give more of yourself and perform at a higher level. They recognize the immense value of consulting with athletes or performers in the shaping of their own destiny.

WE CAN ALL GAIN FROM COACHES WHO HELP US TO FEEL COMPETENT AND CONFIDENT IN OUR ABILITIES TO REACH OUR GOALS.

COMMON COACHING ERRORS

Athletes can improve their performance by preparing themselves for a few common coaching errors. One is some coaches' tendency to become too uptight or wired, in the final preparation phase before an important competition. As an athlete, during the last week or two you might feel as though you are being overloaded or forced to cram for an exam. At a time when you would gain most from a coach who is supportive and calm and boosts your confidence, you might be faced with the opposite. Another common coaching error is a tendency to try to get you "up" before an important competition (for example, "This is a crucial game. Everything is riding on this. All of our work was for this; don't blow it"). If you take this to heart, or do not have a refocusing plan, you could become too stressed or distracted from your best game focus.

Overload in the final preparation phase, excessive technical input, demands for last-minute changes in familiar performance patterns, and an overall increase in stress are major reasons why many athletes and coaches perform below their potential during important events. When you have done a program or performance a hundred times without major problems and then screw up the biggest competition of the year, everyone wonders why. The reason is directly related to overload, heightened demands, and the need to perform under a different set of circumstances—mentally. Two things you don't need at this time are additional demands or stress from your coach.

Another coaching error prevalent at all levels is the failure to give adequate confidence-enhancing feedback. A coach may be quick to tell you that something is wrong, yet not offer specific guidelines about what to focus on to make things right. While pointing out the things that were wrong, he or she may neglect to comment on the good things you have done or the progress you have made. Likewise, you as an athlete may fail to express appreciation for the good things your coach does. Both athletes and coaches need positive feedback and encouragement. We are all human beings first, and most of us really appreciate support and constructive comments.

Positive feedback motivates us, makes us feel good about ourselves and our efforts, and fosters self-confidence. Statements like, "You should be more confident" do nothing to instill additional confidence. But when coaches act and react in ways that demonstrate their belief in us, our confidence is uplifted. Whenever someone cuts us down or dwells on the negative, it undermines our self-confidence, whereas a focus on the positive does just the opposite. Even the best athletes, who feel fairly confident in their abilities, gain from positive feedback, support, and knowing that someone they respect believes in them.

The first step toward personal improvement is to recognize that things can be improved. Then you have several distinct but interrelated choices:

1. Help your coach to understand what works best for you and your performance.
2. Work on improving your own communication skills.
3. Take responsibility to do what is best for you and your performance.
4. Develop your capacity to direct and control your own focus and actions.
5. Draw upon your teammates or those who are closest to you if you need additional support.
6. If all else fails, remember—sometimes the best place to find a helping hand is at the end of your own arm.

Performance is enhanced most readily when coaches and athletes work together to create a positive environment and share responsibility for pursuing the mission and improving ongoing communication. If you want to get the best out of yourself and your situation, it helps immensely to solve those problems in a mature, responsible way.

THE CASE OF KRISTA

A promising young athlete came to see me about quitting. Together we explored her feelings and her options. Within a short time it became clear that her coach was the main source of her stress. She said, "My coach puts me down, discourages me, and screams at me."

Recently Krista attempted a skill, but something was a little off. The exchange went as follows:

Coach: That's wrong! Do it again!

[Krista attempts the skill.]

Coach: It's still wrong . . .you're not trying!

Krista: I'm trying to do it right.

Coach: You are not trying. You won't be able to do it. Forget it.

[Coach turns and walks away.]

Krista related to me what happened next: "I then tried to do it again to show her, but everything went wrong. I went home and decided I'd quit. Now I'm not sure what to do." (Her mother had informed me that tears had been flowing regularly at home lately after practices.) I asked Krista what she had tried to do to improve this situation. "Sometimes I say something back, argue, but it doesn't do any good. The coach just yells more. . . . If the coach is in a really bad mood I just keep my mouth shut, but I'm steaming inside."

I asked, "When the coach does help you perform better or feel better, what does she do?" Krista replied, "She'll be nice to me and tell me, 'You can do it.' She won't scream at me, especially in front of people. She'll smile and help me."

What are Krista's options here?

- She could quit.
- She could find another coach.
- She could try another sport.
- She could hang in there and try to improve her situation.

After we discussed these options, I explained to her, "No one can make these kinds of decisions for you; you must do that for yourself. You are the only person who really knows how you are feeling inside. What I want to do is to help you consider various options. If after exploring some of these options you cannot experience your sport in a more positive or joyful light, then leaving that scene might be the best thing for you. Competition in sport, and preparation for it, should not be something degrading or dreadful. Most of the time it should lift you, make you feel good, and challenge you in positive ways."

Krista decided to continue to practice for another week to try out some improvement strategies. Her approach was two-pronged:

1. Attempt to maintain a more positive perspective in the face of adversity by controlling her own thinking and focus.
2. Try to communicate positively with the coach to positively influence her coach's communication.

POSITIVE SELF-CONTROL

Krista and I talked about her capacity to control her own thinking and focus, and about who really makes us mad. "Does your coach really make you mad," I asked, "or do you get mad because of the way you respond to the things your coach says? Is it absolutely essential that you get mad when these things are said? Isn't shouting at you or being negative a problem or weakness that the coach has, rather than a problem you have? Why should you upset yourself because the coach yells, becomes negative, or has a communication problem?"

We talked about possible reasons why the coach would act that way. Krista said, "I guess she's trying to motivate me, to improve me, but it's the opposite with me . . . when she yells at me I get upset and do worse."

Theresa Grentz, University of Illinois, coaching her team. Remember, every coach has a unique style. Your challenge is to find something valuable that your coach can offer you.

My response was, "Even though you may prefer that the coach communicate with you in a calmer or more constructive way, it may help if you can see the coach's intent in a positive way." We also talked a bit about self-direction. "One of the problems athletes sometimes face when trying to correct errors, make improvements, or perfect new moves is that the coach cannot always see those tiny improvements. It's often viewed as all or none—right or wrong—good or bad—which of course it really isn't. If your coach doesn't acknowledge these little improvements, or doesn't help you embrace the important little steps along the way, somewhere between 'wrong' and 'right,' then do it yourself. You can look for and rejoice in small improvements because they will take you where you want to go."

Krista selected several positive self-control options that she could implement if the tone or content of the coach's communication became a problem. For example: *She's trying to help me improve—this is the only way she knows how to do it. I wonder if she could learn to help me improve with a little less volume. There's no need for me to upset myself because she loses her cool. Relax . . . you can control yourself and your response to her. What is it that she wants me to try? Focus on doing what she is asking you to do so you can do this skill correctly. Smile inside—you are beginning to get things under control.*

POSITIVE COMMUNICATION WITH THE COACH

As athletes, we have to remember that coaches are people too. Most of them are trying to do their best, and they aren't mind readers. You can take some responsibility to communicate with your coach if you want things to improve. I know there are coaches who are sometimes not willing to listen. But sometimes they are, particularly if you can find a quiet time to talk outside of practice or the performance arena. Consider meeting individually with your coach during a relaxed time to talk constructively about what you feel will help you improve. Tell him what makes you work best or most efficiently, what kind of communication you prefer, as well as what upsets you and destroys your workout or performance. You might be able to help each other improve your overall effectiveness.

If meeting with the coach seems initially too threatening, then focus on improving on-site communication. Whenever the coach does something that you find helpful, let him know about it right away. For example, when his feedback is good or constructive, thank him. Tell him it helped you. If he has contributed to a good workout or is giving the kind of feedback that you like, communicate this before leaving practice. Help him to understand how he can help you.

One way to assure the coach that you really are trying and do want to improve is to ask for additional help or for further clarification on his feedback (for example, "Coach, I'd really like to improve this; what specifically should I focus on doing?"). This will help you to get the precise feedback that you want for your skill improvement. The other way to demonstrate your commitment is to practice with full focus and intensity. The more you show your commitment to improve, the more the coach will likely help you.

Krista's challenge was to put some of these strategies to work during the upcoming week. I asked her to keep a daily record of how she felt about her skills and her focus in practice so that we would both know how things were progressing.

Krista also recorded helpful comments made by her coach as well as her response to them. One of her goals here was to try to catch the coach doing something constructive and to let her know it was appreciated.

What follows is a sketch of days 1 and 5 of Krista's first week back at practice.

DAY 1 COMMENTS

- I questioned something I didn't understand ("Do you mean *this*?"). Coach explained.
- I thanked her for the explanation.
- I tried to listen carefully for what she wanted me to do and to look like I was listening.
- I thanked her for the workout.

DAY 5 COMMENTS

- Coach complimented me. I felt great. I thanked her for the compliment and smiled.
- I requested clarification on how to do a certain skill. She responded and showed me how to do it. I thanked her.
- I performed really well.
- Coach joked. I laughed.
- I thanked her for a super workout.

When Krista and I met at the end of the week, it was obvious that her trial week had been a success. About a month later things still seemed to be going well. Krista reported to me, "Coach has been really good lately; she hasn't been getting mad. She doesn't start screaming and yelling for nothing. We talk more, and she even said to come and talk if there's something I'd like to talk about." Communication problems may surface again in the future, but if they do, Krista and her coach should be in a better position to deal with them constructively.

One of the major coaching criticisms relayed to me by experienced athletes is that some of their coaches fail to listen and to act on their input and suggestions. Great coaches will often act on athletes' wisdom, once it is clearly communicated to them, because they respect their experience and want a good performance result. Others will dig in their heels and resist. The resisters are not taking full advantage of the human resources that are available to them.

Even if you meet resistance, you can still take the good things that a coach has to offer. And you can keep working on improving the coach's communication; people do change, miracles sometimes do happen. Your last option, if you are in an incompatible situation, is to consider a coaching change that may bring the joy back to your pursuit and improve the quality of your performance. If you decide to go this route, talk with other athletes about their relationships with prospective coaches, try to visit a couple of workouts run by coaches with whom you think you might be compatible, talk with the ones you like, and then make a decision.

COMMUNICATE YOUR PREFERENCES

It is important to communicate your on-site preferences to your coach so that you optimize your chances of performing well in important events. Good coaches who are really interested in helping each athlete perform to capacity will accept and act on the information because it is in everyone's best interest to do so. Talk with your coach about what you would like her to do, or not do, at the performance site. Be specific in your instructions (for example, "I'd prefer to be left alone"; "Remind me I can do it"; "Talk calmly"; "No last-minute changes"; "Give me corrective feedback only during time-outs").

Too often, important factors that influence performance outcomes are left unmentioned. This is true not only with respect to training sessions but also for competitions. Take, for example, the fact that every single player I interviewed on one professional football team felt that the coach's pregame pep talk, as well as last-minute changes in the game plan, either were a hindrance or did nothing to contribute to the players' mental preparation for the game. The athletes said, "I'm not motivated by it. I know my job; I'm ready, I don't need him to make me ready." "Rah-rah stuff is of no benefit." As one of the more accomplished players stated, "The standard pregame speech that so many of us have heard before is simply not doing the team or individual players any good. However, it may be a method of tension release for the head coach. Having been in the locker room on many occasions, I think it is. If this is so, he should find another way of doing it, away from the players."

Many performers in a variety of disciplines report that their best focus or their confidence may be shaken if too many changes or demands are placed on them just before a game or performance. This is not the time for adding new moves, new strategies, changes within established routines, detailed comments about improving technique, complicated instructions, or even for requiring athletes to sit and listen. Last-minute changes before competition tend to be more detrimental than helpful in almost every sport, unless athletes have been extremely well trained to adapt to them. For certain athletes they can spell disaster. One thing you don't need is lingering thoughts such as *Maybe . . . I'm not as well prepared as I thought. . . . Maybe the coach doesn't have confidence in me. . . . Maybe the coach doesn't have confidence in the game plan we practiced all week. . . . Maybe I (or we) won't be able to perform that well.*

As game time approaches, the coach's job of preparing athletes for the contest has been done. She must now shift gears so as not to interfere with the athletes' last-minute mental preparations. Some athletes appreciate a word of encouragement, a simple reminder, or a reassuring comment, but most prefer to be left alone during their final mental preparations for the event (for example, "Leave me alone so I can concentrate"; "Watch from a distance so as not to distract me"; "I'll call you if I need you"). At high levels in sport, athletes know what they want to do and they have a plan to do it. At all levels in sport, it is the athletes' time to focus in on their performance and the coaches' time to free them to do it.

If you have an assistant coach whose temperament or style of communication fits better with your precompetition needs, request that she interact with you on-site in place of the head coach. I suggested this strategy to some high-level coaches whose team was preparing for an important tournament. The head coach was very high-strung, whereas the assistant coach was calm and low-key. Before the sudden-death elimination match, the two most hyper players on the team interacted only with the calm and reassuring assistant coach. They both played some of the best games of their lives and were instrumental in determining the final outcome, which was in their favor.

Sylvie Bernier also used this best-fit approach when winning her gold medal in diving at the Olympic Games. At Sylvie's request her personal coach, who was at his best during regular training, sat in the stands during the final on-site Olympic practices and competition, while another member of the coaching staff who was calmer, more supportive, and less inclined to give last-minute technical input interacted with her on deck.

It is also helpful to talk with your family members, or the people closest to you, about how you can best support one another as you each pursue your goals. What are your preferences? What is likely to help or hinder your performance? Communicate your mutual preferences in a constructive way and without delay, so that each of you becomes aware of how the other is feeling inside and so each has some positive options to consider when attempting to provide mutual encouragement, support and freedom—at the performance site and away from it.

Respectful communication is a two-way venture. Both you and the person with whom you are interacting are responsible for making it work. Granted, it is not always easy to communicate openly and constructively, especially in conflict situations. I have often debated with myself about whether I should express preferences or discuss certain feelings. However, I know that if I can communicate openly and respectfully, at least there is a possibility of positive change; without communication, things will likely continue on as they are. I simply try to share my perspective and to be constructive, tactful, and honest in doing so. In some situations it is helpful to share your thoughts in writing—for example, through a personal letter or book chapter that outlines the benefits of a certain approach—and then perhaps follow up with a face-to-face discussion about it. Communication is sometimes a delicate process, but in almost all cases it's worth the effort.

CHAPTER 18

BUILDING TEAM HARMONY

One of the most satisfying experiences in sport and the workplace is to be a member of a team that gets along well and works as a cohesive unit. When we live and work together in harmony, the chances of enjoying the journey and achieving our goals are greatly enhanced. Simply making teammates feel appreciated, respected, and accepted can go a long way toward improving team harmony and team performance. This is accomplished through positive communication, mutual acceptance, and genuine encouragement. When we work together to create a positive atmosphere and feeling of unity, better practices or work sessions and higher-quality performances follow.

When sport psychology consultant Cal Botterill studied the link between moods and performance with

IN THE END, IT IS UPON THE QUALITY AND COMMITMENT OF INDIVIDUALS THAT ALL GROUP MOVEMENTS DEPEND.

ROBERTSON DAVIES

highly skilled athletes, he discovered that team harmony was an important factor influencing performance. Each athlete's mood had a direct effect on his or her performance, and what the athletes on the road cited most often as positively influencing their moods was positive interaction with their coaches, roommates, and teammates.

Merely being together at work, practices, competitions, or in social settings like team parties does not necessarily increase mutual liking or harmony among team members. For harmony to develop, individuals must commit to a common mission or goal, or be linked in some interdependent way so that they rely on one another and help one another in the pursuit of that goal.

Harmony grows when you take the time to stop long enough to listen to others and when they listen to you; when you respect their feelings and they respect yours; when you accept their differences and they accept yours; when you choose to help them and they help you. Harmony is rooted in mutual trust and respect.

When you know that someone needs you, cares about you, appreciates you, respects you, believes in you, and accepts you—with your imperfections—harmony is nurtured. When we help others and they help us, we begin to appreciate each other. When we get past the surface and begin to understand another person's problems, challenges, or perspectives in a more intimate way, we feel closer to or more connected with them.

Several teams I have worked with have had their fair share of disharmony and interpersonal conflicts—including members feeling ignored or left out, athletes feeling that the coach had no respect for them, people refusing to room with each other or withdrawing emotionally or physically from the group, and an actual shoving match on-site before an international competition. It is rare that teammates or coaches intentionally create conflict or resentment, or set out to hurt others' feelings. No one gains from that process; it usually puts both parties through unpleasant turmoil and creates stress that ultimately affects team performance negatively. A lack of commitment to an overriding team mission, a lack of awareness of other people's feelings, or a misinterpretation of actions or intentions is at the root of many interpersonal conflicts.

Most of us would agree that harmony is preferable to disharmony within families, relationships, sport teams, and work teams. Sometimes there is natural harmony or compatibility within a relationship or team, but often there is not. This is when a commitment is required from everyone involved to put the bigger mission, or goal, above the conflict or disharmony. The team mission or common goal must be placed above everything else, with everyone working hard and supporting one another to achieve a worthy, higher-level goal. Remaining flexible, finding good qualities in teammates, and working together to accomplish mutually beneficial goals puts the team on the path to harmony and excellence.

Open communication is an important step in preventing and solving potential problems. It is difficult to be responsive to another's needs or feelings when you do not know what they are. It is difficult to respect another's perspective if you do not understand what it is or where it came from. The time to commit to the team mission and to constructive communication is now. Solve problems when they are small rather than waiting until they have grown out of proportion. This is important both in sport and in other aspects of life.

Imagine that you are going on an extended space voyage to another planet. You are restricted to living, working, and training in close proximity to your teammates within a confined space about the size of an average office. You must remain in this space several years. There is no chance of leaving until the mission is completed. Living and working in harmony would become critical to your survival, the survival of your teammates, and the mission itself. What would you do to avoid conflict or maintain some sense of harmony on a mission like this? Who would you want with you on this mission?

Crew members for long-duration space missions have to be well selected for compatibility and adaptability—otherwise communication might break down and destroy the essential human links that would otherwise allow them to succeed. On sport teams and workplace teams, it is rare that members are chosen based on their natural compatibility, or their ability to adapt and to work well with others. On our earthly teams it is unlikely that we will have a natural fit among all team members—so making the best of what we have and adapting in positive ways to the situation we are facing become critical parts of completing our mission successfully.

Compared to our long-distance voyagers, we do have several advantages. We do not have to leave behind our family, friends, and everything on our planet that is familiar or comforting for years at a time. We have the advantage of being able to step away from our teammates, enjoy a beautiful natural world, and rejoice in many other simple pleasures. This makes our task easier and allows us to return to our mission on a daily basis with renewed energy and greater tolerance for those with whom we are linked on this mission.

Whenever people are linked together in pursuit of challenging, mutually beneficial goals, several action points become essential for individual and group success.

- Find the good qualities in each team member.
- Recognize the good things each can do or contribute.
- Commit to remain positive through adversity; all challenges, great and small, demand overcoming adversity or obstacles.
- Embrace the challenge.
- Focus on doing your job the best you can.
- Help each other accomplish the team goal.
- Put the mission above the conflict or obstacle.
- Remember—when you carry a positive perspective, you can tolerate or work with almost anyone for short-duration missions.

If you believe that someone on the team or in the organization is doing something that is negatively affecting the team's performance, consider talking with that person—directly or through a team representative (for example, the team captain, an assistant coach or manager, or a trusted staff member). Respectfully express both your concerns and your appreciation for the good things that are happening. It is important for team members to know which of their actions help, and which needlessly hinder, team performance. Your actions may help others to communicate in ways that enhance team harmony and team performance.

RESOLVING CONFLICTS

When a communication problem exists, even though one party may have been more responsible for creating it, both usually end up sharing the responsibility to implement a workable solution. There are three ongoing ways to reduce conflict and improve team harmony that need attention from coaches and teammates alike:

1. Work on improving your own communication skills. Set a goal to become a better listener, and work on expressing feelings respectfully and constructively.
2. Work on improving your skills at respectfully helping others and respectfully receiving help. Set a goal to give assistance

more readily and to receive suggestions more openly and enthusiastically.

3. Work on improving your own emotional control. Set a goal to focus and act in ways that let you and your teammates achieve the best results, and work on refocusing to stay positive or constructive when things don't go your way.

Teammates can often help one another learn, provide positive challenges or examples for one another, constructively analyze one another's performances, provide a lift or word of encouragement when needed, and share perspectives on how to improve team harmony or focus in a way that benefits all team members. If your teammates know what helps you prepare mentally for your challenges or performances, they will be in a position to learn from it, to help set the stage for your best performance, or at least to not inadvertently interfere. Positive communication and meaningful feedback among teammates and between coaches and performers is extremely important in terms of attaining our best possible performance and personal well-being. How many times did this kind of communication happen today? Can you make it happen more often?

The following are additional suggestions offered by athletes for promoting positive interaction:

- Get to know your teammates well.
- Talk with your teammates.
- Listen to your teammates.
- Avoid put-downs.
- Decide that you will get along.
- Take responsibility for yourself, doing what you can to improve the situation.
- Encourage each other.
- Accept individual differences.
- Include everyone.
- Show others that you care.

Harmony is a worthy goal in itself because of the way it makes you and other people feel. But it is also important because it leads to improved performance for all team members.

Making Differences Work for You

There are vast individual differences among members of all teams ... different experiences, different perspectives, different responses to stress, different ways of focusing or coping with distractions, different strengths. These differences can work to your advantage and make you stronger as a team if you are willing to learn from each other, to work together, and to share your strengths. No coach or performer knows everything. But when teams of people put their heads together, they can know almost everything that is important for team success. One veteran performer may have 10 or 20 years of rich experience, but as a group you probably have over 200.

On many teams, most athletes do things pretty much on their own, keeping many of their good thoughts and insights to themselves. Although there are many individual strengths, there is not much sharing of strengths or strategies for excelling.

Your team will become much stronger if you follow these steps:

1. Decide as individuals and as a group that you really want to excel, or to be the best you can be.

2. Help one another excel by sharing your strengths and your visions of how to improve or become your best. Let me give you some examples: One player can remain incredibly focused in pressure situations, another is superb at preparing to take advantage of opponents' weaknesses, a third can stay highly motivated in practices and bring a high level of intensity to every shift and every game, and a fourth can maintain a positive focus after a setback or when coming back from behind. If you can discuss how various team members approach these and other important challenges (for example, how do you get yourself to focus for a full game, or to react to errors or criticism constructively?), you can all gain something. No one is totally strong in all areas. We all have room for improvement, technically, physically, tactically, mentally, or emotionally. If a teammate wants to improve in some area, you or someone who is strong in that area can offer help in a nonthreatening way—saying, for example, "It may not work for you, but I find this works for me." As a team line or playing unit you can discuss your *collective* strengths and specific areas to improve. Together you can review opponents' strengths and weaknesses and make tactical suggestions that may be of value to individual players. Regular discussions that are open and constructively oriented among team members before and after games or performances can do wonders for team morale and overall performance.

Working together to create a positive atmosphere and feeling of unity can result in higher-quality performances.

3. Encourage one another for genuine efforts to make improvements and support one another for making any steps in the right direction. In performance situations, physical skills cease to be enough. Your thoughts and emotions must be working for you. Your task becomes much easier if your teammates and coach are also working for you, or at least not against you.

BUILDING RAPPORT

What follows is an account of just one of many instances where I've been asked to help resolve conflicts within a team. Coach X calls me with some urgent concerns about interpersonal conflicts on the team. The atmosphere is filled with tension, practices are degenerating, spirits are low. Conflicts exist between the coach and certain athletes, as well as among some team members. The problem has escalated to the point where practices are being ruined and many people leave practice feeling emotionally upset. The coach is fed up. The athletes are fed up. Coach X describes the situation as desperate.

"Can you help?" is the resounding echo that reverberates through the phone. "I don't know," I say, "but I can come over and give it a try."

How would you go about trying to help? How could your own practice environment be made more positive and productive for both athletes and coaches?

I begin by asking the coach and each athlete a few questions:

- What is the main reason you come to practice?
- If you could change anything you wanted about practice, what would you change?
- Is there anything the coach or other athletes could do to make you feel or work better in practice? What about at competitions?
- What would make practice a happier and more productive place to be?
- When the coach is at his best, what does he do?
- When the coach is at his worst, what does he do?
- What are two things in your life that you like to do best?
- What are your overall goals in your sport?

After reviewing the responses to each question, I speak to the group openly to share their overall views:

■ Everyone, athletes and coach, says that his or her involvement in this sport is one of the things in life that he or she likes best. You all want to improve your skills and to have positive and more productive practices. You feel great when you learn a new move or perfect an old one, and so does the coach. Your overall goals are similar, but sometimes you get in each other's way, and as a result nobody achieves their goals. At those times, nobody enjoys being here and nobody learns very much.

The quickest way you can all have happier and more productive practices is to work together and help one another. What exactly can each of you do to help make that happen? Well, on the basis of your responses to my questions, I have created some "happy workout suggestions."

These workout suggestions can be written on index cards, and you can distribute them to the athletes and the coach as helpful reminders, or cue cards, for subsequent practices. The goal is to do as many of the actions listed on one card as possible in one practice session, and to do the remaining ones at the next practice.

Sample Cue Cards

Coach Reminders I
1. Absolutely no yelling—no matter what happens, stay cool.
2. Smile—show you are in a good mood. Let players know you are happy to be there.
3. Point out what is good, then correct constructively.
4. After giving correction, briefly explain why.
5. Say something positive not related to the sport.
6. Be encouraging and reassuring with words and actions.

Coach Reminders II
1. Give positive feedback every chance you get.
2. Lighten up a little—loosen up.
3. Give specific instruction and encouragement.
4. Tell the athletes what they did well tonight.
5. Say goodnight and leave the gym happy.

Coach Reminders III
1. Show that you care and want each athlete there.
2. Say hello to everyone sometime today.
3. Give everyone some individual feedback sometime today.
4. Listen closely when athletes give input or express a feeling.
5. Respect and act upon the athletes' input.
6. Feel good about your own progress.

Athlete Reminders I
1. Smile and say hello to everybody.
2. Stop, look (establish eye contact), and listen when the coach is correcting you. Make a real effort to correct the skill.
3. Be ready to go—stand tall.
4. Come to practice with all the personal equipment you might need.
5. Help a teammate today.
6. If your coach or another athlete has been helpful, tell him or her that you appreciate it.
7. Set a good example by approaching skills and drills with full focus and good intensity.

Athlete Reminders II

1. Think positive thoughts today—make someone else feel good too.
2. Ask the coach what you should do to make something better, then really try.
3. Remind yourself that your coach is trying to help you reach your goals.
4. Give 100 percent focus and effort today.
5. Watch a teammate and compliment him or her on something she does well.
6. If anyone is getting discouraged, try to cheer him or her up.
7. Tell the coach that he really helps bring out your best when he respects and encourages you.
8. Remember upcoming events and important dates.

Obviously, a coach cannot give individualized feedback to all athletes at the same time, particularly in sports where there are many players or several events going on at once. However, teammates can watch, correct, advise, and encourage each other. Fellow athletes can often see and understand, better than anyone, what you are doing, not doing, or what might help you get better.

One activity that I have found to be very successful with teams of experienced athletes, classmates, workmates, or families involves simply sharing the good qualities we see in our teammates. The way we often do this is as follows: First, write each team member's name on the top of a piece of paper. Then ask everyone on the team to write down one thing they like, admire, appreciate, respect, or enjoy about that person. The sheets of paper are passed around the room, from person to person, and each adds his or her positive comments about that particular teammate. This activity can also be done verbally, but writing things down adds a special dimension. Everyone leaves the room with a collection of very uplifting comments from their teammates, which they can post somewhere or refer back to when they need a little lift. Positive comments by teammates are often shared in this context that would otherwise never be shared. It definitely feels good to read over these comments.

FOLLOW-UP

To find out how interactions were affected by these attempts to improve team harmony, we observed Coach X's team before and after the intervention. The rate of positive verbal interaction (for example, praise, compliments, and encouragement) doubled, and, most important, negative criticism (for example, yelling and put-downs) was almost completely eliminated.

The coach commented, "Everything is working out much better now. Everyone seems to be more happy and relaxed. All the athletes seem to be really working and trying hard."

The moral of this story or chapter is that everyone on a team, even in individual sports, is linked together like a family. What you do and how you respond to others has an effect on how others feel and how they respond to you. To make this kind of family happy and productive, each of us has to do our part. It may take a little extra effort in the beginning, but it's worth it in the end. When we encourage each other, help each other, listen to each other, support each other, and interact with each other in positive ways, everybody will be happier, work harder, and learn more. We will all enjoy being in that setting more and leave the team as better performers and better people.

CHAPTER 19

LEARNING FROM SETBACKS

LOSING IN SPORT

I remember my first experience at the U.S. Eastern Intercollegiate Gymnastics Championships particularly well. It was my second year at Syracuse University, where I had accepted a gymnastics scholarship after having won almost every gymnastic competition I had entered as a youngster and a teenager. I had worked especially hard during the summer and the regular season to regain lost ground that resulted from an injury sustained during my first year of university competition. The injury had sidelined me for the season. I wanted to prove something to myself and those around me, and I also wanted to feel worthy of my scholarship. I concentrated my effort on the trampoline, as this was the first event I could get back to after my injury.

A REFINED ABILITY TO LEARN FROM FAILURE AND TO GROW THROUGH LOSSES IS NECESSARY TO ACHIEVE EXCELLENCE IN ANY HUMAN ENDEAVOR.

During the season I consistently outscored my competitors and felt that I had a really good shot at winning the title. Actually, I thought I would win it, and so did most of my teammates. I had prepared well and was ready—so I thought. I remember hearing my name called, jumping up on the tramp, bouncing high into the air, throwing one trick, and landing on the springs. That was the end of my routine, the end of my hopes—the end of my dreams.

What a way to end the season! I was really quite upset. All I wanted to do was to get out of there. I didn't want to talk to anyone; I didn't want to eat; and I wasn't looking forward to responding to the standard questions like "Did you win?" or "What happened?" when I returned to campus. I was down for about two weeks. It isn't important now, but at the time it was probably the most important thing in my world. There are much bigger losses in life that eventually put these in perspective.

Significant losses have a way of colliding with our self-esteem. The vibrations can result in self-doubt, self-damnation, worry, and even guilt. Though these thoughts can become overwhelming, there is no reason they have to be. It's helpful to remember that this loss is not you—it is something that you are currently experiencing. You have so many more qualities within yourself, and you mean so much more to others than this loss does. You can deal with the experience of loss and grow from it. The hurtful feelings will fade—they always do. Even though you have lost, you have gained something from the experience, and you are a stronger, wiser person—perhaps even a better performer—for it.

Now what did I accomplish by coming down on myself, by denying myself enjoyment, by punishing myself? I had failed to meet an important goal that I felt had been a realistic one. I had carried out one of the worst performances of my career when it was most important for me to do my best. However, I hadn't tried to do poorly. The fact that I was trying so hard probably contributed to my problem in the first place. I was a little too pumped up. As a result, I threw the first trick so hard that I overrotated and headed for the springs. Is this a just reason to be mad at myself?

That particular loss turned out to be a golden opportunity to learn something that is difficult to learn under any other circumstances. I was disappointed, but it wasn't the end of the world. It didn't mean that I was a worthless person. It had nothing to do with my overall human value. It had to do with my ability to perform a certain kind of skill, under specific conditions, in a certain frame of mind.

I learned that I had to be a little calmer in championship events, and I began to experiment with strategies to accomplish this. I also learned to wait until everything was centered and felt right before starting the routine.

I finally did begin to get my head together. I began to look for positive lessons from an unfortunate experience. I asked myself, *What did I learn about myself? What did I learn about those around me? What did I learn about performing in stressful circumstances? What did I learn that can help me in the future?* Only then did losing become a positive learning experience. It was largely because of that learning that I was able to go back the following year and win the eastern intercollegiate title and the NCAA regional title as well. From that time on, the perspective that I took into sport and life allowed me to gain something from the experience itself, regardless of numerical outcomes or the achievement of preset goals.

Even the greatest performers fail, but they have developed strategies to learn and benefit from these experiences. They certainly don't like falling short of a goal, so they try to put it in perspective, and do a careful evaluation to prevent similar occurrences in the future. They may conclude that this time, this particular approach or game plan didn't work, or their focus wasn't fully absorbed in the task, or the cards weren't falling in their favor that day. They don't tear themselves apart for long in response to loss—they simply prepare better or differently for the next opportunity, which may be in or outside of a sporting context.

To lose is to be human . . . and we are all human. Every thinking, feeling, living person experiences loss. No one escapes it—not even the greatest of the greats. "Your task is to make the journey from immediate loss to eventual gain as rapidly, smoothly and comfortably as possible" (Colgrove, Bloomfield, and McWilliams 1993, 22).

We tend to be most susceptible to feeling down when we expect to do well and do poorly instead, when we expect to win and we lose, when we expect love or acceptance and experience rejection. In such cases, sometimes our expectations have been unrealistic; sometimes we have not prepared or focused as well as we could have, and we can work on this; and sometimes we have done everything in our power to make things happen (given the constraints of our time and resources) and, for reasons totally beyond our control, events do not go as we hoped or planned. It is important to recognize the difference between circumstances that are within our control and those that are beyond it. "Fight for the highest attainable aim but never put up resistance in vain" (Selye 1978, 300).

There is no advantage in dwelling on the negative or on things that are beyond our control. It is better to use your limited energy constructively by directing it toward positive ends. Loss can make you feel miserable, inadequate, or helpless. But it can also challenge you to draw upon your strengths; persist through the obstacles; get to know yourself better; examine your priorities; put things in perspective; and reflect on where you are going, why, and how. A time of loss can widen your perspective or redirect your course, in

The lessons you take from loss can be valuable in helping you learn to perform better.

sport or in life. As unpleasant as it may be, loss can result in your learning how to better prepare for, influence, avoid, embrace, or cope with situations that may arise in the future. If you can draw anything good out of your loss, or put what remains in perspective, loss has a positive side; it is no longer totally hopeless.

The route to personal excellence and meaningful self-growth is full of ups and downs; progressions and regressions; great leaps forward, backslides, and plateaus. But as long as the overall direction is up, you will ascend the mountain—and there are many mountains to climb in this life, all of different textures.

Life is a constant process of transition and adaptation; the better you can cope, the happier, healthier, and more fulfilled you will be. If you can view difficulties and setbacks as a challenge, as a test of your inner strength, as an opportunity for personal growth, then you can turn these experiences into advantages. Finding the lessons in loss has an interesting way of putting you back in control.

Chapter 20

Preventing Overload and Embracing Life

Overload. Every time it happens, I know it. I feel myself being pulled in too many directions at once. I start moving faster mentally, and my guts tie up in a knot as I think about how I can meet everyone's demands, including my own. I become more irritable toward other people, especially those I love, not because they are the ones making the demands but because they just happen to be around. Once I settle down and become more relaxed, I reflect and put things back in perspective; I don't like being in that overload state even temporarily, I don't like feeling rushed, and think that it is ridiculous to get caught up in it. So I decide that I am not going to let that happen again.

I try to prevent overload by planning meetings, major commitments, and other scheduled activities so that they are not back-to-back, with one

THE GREATEST GIFT IN LIFE IS FINDING HARMONY WITHIN YOURSELF.

still incomplete while others are starting. If I feel an overload coming on I remind myself, *Take a few minutes to relax—it won't do you any good to get yourself upset over this; if you don't finish this now, you will finish it later; you can only do so much.* That reminder in itself can put me in a healthier frame of mind. Sometimes I will shut the door and lie down on the floor in my office and just relax for 5 or 10 minutes and put things back in perspective before moving on to another challenge or task.

From time to time, I still find myself overwhelmed by too many demands. Most of the time, though, I can predict how much I can handle comfortably and adjust my pace before getting into trouble. This often means saying no to people, situations, or requests, but it means saying yes to life. We have to remind ourselves continually to direct the course of our own lives, rather than let others direct our lives for us.

As you begin to gain profile as an athlete, performer, coach, teacher, musician, entertainer, writer, or a person skilled in any field, more demands are placed on you. The better you get or the higher the profile, the greater the demands. Prior to and following major events, top performers face all kinds of additional demands. Everyone wants a piece of you, and if you give them all what they want, there will be nothing left for you or your loved ones. At times, there are too many requests—from sponsors, media people, and the public, for interviews, appearances, responses to calls, e-mail, and so on—and not enough time or energy in any one life to fulfill them.

If you find yourself in a situation where there are more demands than there is time to fulfill them, you must take control. Decide how much you can realistically handle and how much you want to take on. Maybe you feel you can handle two outside requests, appearances, interviews, social events, or talks a month, but none during your busiest times or before important events. You may find that you cannot answer all your e-mail, letters, and calls; so you can either get someone to help you carry that load or not answer them. It is crucial to set priorities and follow them. Otherwise you can be sucked dry by people who demand a lot but don't give much in return; who really don't care about you as a person; or who don't realize how difficult it is to keep up your current commitments to your work, training, or loved ones, let alone to meet outside requests.

A little overload, or even a lot, every now and then won't kill you—but a continuous diet of overload and stress can destroy the quality of your health, your performance, your relationships, and your life. When high-performance people take on additional outside demands, they often find that they are no longer respecting the patterns that allow them to perform so well. Even if they continue to work or train as hard, the extra demands sap their energy, compromise important rest time, and introduce a higher level of imbalance into their lives.

Most people never come close to gaining the profile of an athletic champion, a well-known actor, or a celebrated musician, but all of us face times when the demands of life seem greater than our capacity to meet them. This is common for university students, parents with young children, teachers, coaches, business executives, and performers in a variety of fields. To avoid overload, you must first think about priorities. What are your priorities at this point in life? What are your priorities for this day in your work or performance domain? What are your priorities for this day outside of your work or performance domain? How many additional commitments can you take on and still execute these priorities with quality and connection?

The first line of defense against an imbalanced or stressful lifestyle is a plan to prevent overload and embrace simple joys. Set some guidelines to ensure that you schedule enough time for quality rest, quality preparation, and enjoyment in living. Then follow those guidelines! You can do a lot more quality work within a shorter period of time if you are well rested and in a positive state of mind. Try to maintain a sense of harmony in your life and adjust your pace if it leads to disharmony. Learn to relax in the face of stress and find joyful ways to recover from the stresses you face.

Worrying about deadlines or about being late or not ready for something takes time, energy, and focus away from your tasks and creates stress. Be realistic in making additional commitments—that is, overestimate rather than underestimate the amount of time, energy, and work involved in getting something done with quality. Start preparing earlier to meet deadlines by setting short-term goals. Leave early enough for appointments, classes, meetings, or practices to arrive early without having to rush. Accept the fact that at a certain time you will have to stop working on one mission to successfully complete another.

Challenging or creative work often occurs in waves—this day or week may be extremely heavy, which is fine as long as tomorrow or next week is light. When possible, spread out your workload over a reasonable timeframe and leave spaces for simple joys between them. Accepting a series of back-to-back commitments for a time that seems far in the future can come back to haunt you when that time becomes the present. Set priorities so that you say yes only to those things you really want to do. Choose to do more things that lift you, and fewer things that drain you.

Before saying yes to anything that makes additional demands on your limited time, think about what the gain will be and what the cost will be in time and energy. You can bet that any given task will take longer than you have been told. A "10-minute" interview often ends up taking at least an hour out of your life—talking on the phone, making arrangements, thinking about what to say, getting there, waiting until everyone is set up and ready to go, getting home, and so on. In agreeing to a request, indicate exactly how much time and commitment you are willing, and not willing, to give. Set your conditions and call the shots before you accept.

If you are not sure whether you want to do it, my advice is simple: Don't! Your life is not likely to suffer, or be any less fulfilling, for not doing it. It will probably be better, because you will have a little more time for you and the things you love to do. So if you are not sure whether this additional demand will help you live your life more fully, at least delay committing yourself. Give yourself a few days to assess the relevancy of the request to see how it fits with your overall schedule and priorities.

Remember the word *no*. It is sometimes hard to say, but it is often the only way to maintain quality in your performance and preserve a balanced or harmonious lifestyle. I have found that being respectful and honest in denying requests reduces my load and my level of stress (for example, "I would like to do it, but I have so many commitments already that I simply can't fit it in and still maintain any quality in my life").

If you are a busy person, and you want to say yes more often, it should be for things that are personally uplifting (for example, time for you, time with family or friends, or doing things you really enjoy or find exciting or relaxing). Balanced excellence is not a question of working any less diligently while you are working or training, it is a question of lightening your load and relaxing more fully outside of training or working hours.

Let's say that you are already pulled in many directions and are feeling stressed. For the moment, avoid additional demands. Find a quiet place to escape where you don't have to answer to anyone. Short timeouts can really bring things back into perspective and put you back in control of your life. Allow yourself a little time to relax, to embrace some simple joys, and to regain a more positive perspective. Once you feel in a better frame of mind, try to meet your demands as best you can, taking one little step at a time.

Taking a timeout from a busy schedule can bring things back into perspective and put you back in control of your life.

Even if you are late for a deadline, don't blow it out of proportion. This time it will be late. It is not going to kill you or them. Relax. Slow down. Learn something from this experience about controlling your own schedule and planning your time to prevent it from repeating itself. The world won't end if you miss this deadline. It is not worth upsetting yourself. Take a walk. Do something you really enjoy. Embrace a few moments of silence. Enjoy a few minutes of your life. Draw out the lessons and move on.

Listen to yourself. Listen to your body. Slow down and relax. You know when you're getting overloaded. Physical signs, emotional signs, and changes in feelings tell you. You may start to feel tense, grumpy, negative, or irritated by things that normally do not bother you, or you may begin to feel drained, easily distracted, unmotivated, or out of control. Your body and your emotions are telling you to slow down, but you are not listening. If you begin to heed your personal signs and relax your pace before the overload, you can save yourself a lot of grief. There is no need to rush everywhere and through everything. Take it easy. Move in a confident, unhurried fashion. Focus on connecting fully with your experiences. When you sit down to talk with someone, relax, listen, and then relax again for a few moments before responding. Slow down when you walk or drive from one place to another. Walk relaxed. Run relaxed. If the phone rings, relax for a few rings before responding, or if you would prefer to avoid additional demands, don't answer it at all. Relax in the shower, in front of a fire, in the sauna. Eat relaxed and drink more slowly. After eating, take a little time to do nothing but fully enjoy some quiet time alone or with your loved ones. Relax a bit every day by doing something you love, listening to music, getting yourself into a positive or relaxing environment, relaxing the muscles in your body, stretching out on the grass, or doing whatever makes you feel good. Try to relax more fully in stressful settings. If necessary, take a five-minute timeout from the stress-related situation to relax, to be alone, or to regroup.

If people you love may be suffering or feeling neglected because of your overload, talk with them about your feelings. Reassure them that you love them. Let them know that what is upsetting you is your overload, and that you are trying to get it under control. They will appreciate knowing that they are not the cause of your short temper, anger, or unhappiness. Talking with them may even reduce your load and help you to cope in more constructive ways. The long-range challenge is to prevent overload, to embrace the different loves of your life more fully, and to live your life more joyfully. This can begin today.

- Decide to live this day free from worry or stress.
- Decide to live it free from anger.
- Decide to live it free from overload.
- Plan to do something this day you really enjoy outside of your work.
- Plan to do something you love to do with your family.
- Plan to do something with quality and complete connection.
- Just one day, decide to live it fully.

Chapter 21

From Hero to Zero and Back

At some points in your life, when things are going very well, you might feel a little bit like a hero. At other points, when things aren't going so well, you may feel more like a zero. This shift in feelings often occurs in major transitions or during times of uncertainty.

A medalist at the Olympic Games was convinced that excelling in her sport was the only really important thing in her life. All those other people out there (outside the training regimen) "weren't doing anything important." As she expressed it, "Then I stopped competing and became one of them." It took her years to regain perspective and confidence in herself as a person.

If you believe that you are important only because of your performance in a particular domain, then what is left when you are no longer

THE CHALLENGE IS NOT ONLY TO PURSUE EXCELLENCE, BUT TO DO SO WHILE EMBRACING THE REST OF YOUR LIFE.

performing as well in that domain? An all-consuming marriage to sport, school, or work to the exclusion of everything leads to imbalance. The breakup of this kind of marriage is difficult to cope with, especially when you leave feeling like, *I'm finished; I'm no longer good enough to be here, and without this I'm nothing.*

Growing apart from one's sport or performance domain certainly doesn't have to produce these feelings, but it does far more often than is necessary. All dedicated performers have a common commitment to fulfill a dream of excellence. But it is not necessary to shut out the rest of your life. For most athletes, sport is the main focus in life, particularly during their years of greatest passion and improvement. However, it is important to distinguish between "the most important thing" and "the only thing." Both allow you to pursue excellence, but only one allows you to do so without sacrificing the rest of your life. Something will suffer when one phase of your life, such as sport or work, weighs too heavily for too long a time. It may be your passion, your overall growth, your family life, your relationships, your health, your perspective—or something else. When you no longer look forward to the dawning of each day, when you forget how to play in joyful ways, when the inner smile leaves your life, something is out of balance.

It is possible to pursue high levels of excellence while still embracing other important parts of your life, if a commitment to balance is built into your vision and plan. Balance is finding beauty, passion, and meaning in the different loves of your life and living those loves—every day or every opportunity. It is not a question of equal time, but rather making the best of the time you have and connecting fully with each experience. Balance requires that you continue to embrace the playful side of life, find special time for yourself, and enjoy moments of relaxed intimacy with others. Balance or imbalance emerges from the perspective you carry. You find balance and harmony when you embrace simple joys; when you accept that you are worthy, valued, or loved apart from your performance; and when you respect the different loves of your life. This vision of excellence allows you to give and gain more from life in the long run.

THE DECISION TO RETIRE

People who emerge the best adjusted in the years following retirement from active competition are those who are able to attain a sense of balance or harmony during their competitive years. No doubt, sport or performance received their highest commitment for a good portion of their lives to that point, but other pursuits were not considered without value. Important relationships and other joyful pursuits remained alive and important, while necessarily receiving less time during those periods of highest commitment. The challenge in achieving balance and excellence is to establish priorities for different times and phases in your life, and shift focus into and out of each priority as you see fit. You gain immeasurably from committing yourself to the pursuit of excellence, but you gain equally from respecting some of the other loves in your life. The pursuit you are now engaged in is but one of many of life's wonderful adventures.

All athletes, from high school participants to Olympic and professional champions, are destined to experience declines in performance and profile in competitive sport. The uncertainty that accompanies transition out of high-performance sport may generate stress or fear. This is true as well for other transitions, including students leaving college hoping to move into the workplace. Ultimately the challenge is to embrace transitions; they are inevitable and provide many new opportunities and adventures. When the need for one set of skills is gone or reduced, you are not less of a person. You simply channel some of your strengths into other meaningful domains or pursuits. What you have learned from your journey can help you continue to contribute and grow for the rest of your life.

To quote an athlete who had a difficult transition:

■ My sport and competing was my life. One evening I had had enough and decided that the sport circus was not worth my efforts any longer. In the beginning I felt like a failure. I couldn't see daily success in everyday life. The large step back into normal life was difficult because of a lack of education, no profession, and no intimate relationships. On the positive side, I was a person again, not just an athlete. I had a chance to go back to school, I had more time for friends and for developing meaningful relationships. I underwent a change in values, got out of the rat race of having to be successful in order to be happy. What I would suggest to make retirement easier for others is to lead a more normal life (for example, continue with your education, maintain a social life and home life, and get involved in some other activities). Then the transition will not be so traumatic.

Although for some athletes or performers the retirement experience is difficult, others have a relatively easy transition. One athlete said, "I thought it was easy. I had other hobbies, a career, and a personal life that could easily be expanded and improved." People who have relatively fluid transition experiences seem to have one or more of the following things going for them:

- They have been respecting other parts of their life during their competitive years.
- They have meaningful options to consider upon retirement.
- They have the complete support of at least one important person upon retirement or immediately afterward (a parent, coach, close friend, or loved one).

Following are some suggestions from athletes who have been through transitions. Before the retirement decision:

- Find a coach who respects you as a whole person rather than just as a performer. A more personal approach can help you leave feeling worthwhile after many years of dedicated training.
- Remember your personal development through education, work, family, and friends is an integral part of your overall training program.
- Take some time to relax and enjoy something outside of your sport or performance domain.
- Assess what you want from your sport or performance domain and from your life. Get to know yourself well enough to decide what is best for you.
- Change your routine in the off-seasons. Go to school, take some courses, spend some time in nature, do something else you enjoy.
- Make time for meaningful experiences other than training and performing. Schedule other activities into your overall program (for example, time for you, time with others, time for simple joys or educational activities).
- Focus some of your energy in new areas of interest while still actively competing so that if it interests you, the option is there for continuation or expansion after retirement.

- Think of transitions as great opportunities to enter a new phase of your life, to learn something new, to grow, to develop, to contribute in other areas, to embrace life.

After the retirement decision:

- Once your transition decision has been made, let your family and friends know that it would be really great to have their support.
- Consider other interesting pursuits, training, adventures, or opportunities in areas where you already have strengths or in any other area that really interests you.
- Stay actively involved in sports, fitness, or outdoor activities for the sheer joy of it. Participate in self-paced activities, or get involved in "veterans" events. Adjust your goals accordingly.
- If possible, arrange for a sharing of experiences with others going through a similar transition. Exchange thoughts and feelings about your experiences and about adapting to a different lifestyle.

A transition can be an opportunity to try a new activity.

- If things are getting you down, discuss your concerns with someone close to you, or see a counselor for personal, educational, career, business, or leisure planning. Counselors are available on virtually all university campuses.

POSITIVE ADAPTATION

What will happen to you when you move from a position of security, familiarity, and competence (or at least recognition as an athlete, student, or performer) to what at first might appear to be nothing? If you sit around telling yourself that you are incapable of doing anything else, or dwell on how lousy things are, how great things used to be, or how the system screwed you, you will likely talk yourself into a state of inaction. However, if you view this transition as an opportunity to grow in other areas, to expand your horizons in meaningful ways, and learn to recognize that the admiration of others is simply not necessary for a rich and fulfilling life, then the passage will be much more positive.

The mental skills and perspectives that you have learned and perfected while pursuing your goals will give you one of the most valuable contributions that sport or performance pursuits can offer. These mental skills will ease your transition and increase your chances of ongoing growth and lifetime satisfaction.

In all likelihood, you still have much of your life ahead of you to direct as you please. It's not what's gone, but what is left that counts. You can pursue and enjoy all sorts of things that you were unable to fully embrace before, mainly because so much time and energy were concentrated on one focus. I never once skied in all those years I was competing in gymnastics. The seasons conflicted; besides, I felt obligated to avoid injury. But after I stopped competing in gymnastics, I discovered that I love skiing and spending time in beautiful outdoor settings. You'll have ample opportunity to apply some of your positive perspectives and focusing skills to other meaningful pursuits. Positive thinking, goal setting, stress control, focusing, and refocusing can be readily transferred to all domains. In addition, if you plan well, you will have more time to spend with people you care about.

Some athletes do feel bitter and negative about their sports careers after they are over. A few feel that as a result of all their striving, they have missed some important things in life, such as full involvement with their families, intimate relationships, enjoyable socialization with friends, or educational or occupational development. Others who leave with bitterness feel that they have been pawns, that they have been used or abused and then cast aside like garbage. People in their lives who had appeared to care so much in the past seemed quick to divert their attention elsewhere when the "machine" could no longer contribute to their ends.

It is true that certain people may try to use and abuse you for their own selfish ends. They may see you strictly as a performance object, and when that object is no longer performing or following orders, it is of absolutely no value. This tells you more about those people than about yourself. Their insensitivity need not affect the way you see yourself as a person, unless you choose to accept their distorted view of humanity. Fortunately, a genuine sense of caring lives within most athletes and coaches.

One way to take control of your own life is to make some choices for yourself. Establish your own goals. Then, in pursuing your goals, try to get the best out of yourself and bring out the best in those around you. Think about who can help you and how—so you can better understand and utilize their strengths. If necessary, find a more compatible coach or more uplifting people.

If you start to get down on yourself for not being as good as you should be, as good as you used to be, for going downhill physically, for feeling useless, and so on—think back. Think back to when you were a beginner in your sport or performance domain. You are a lot more skilled now than you were then, in a lot of ways. Yet you were worthwhile then. Why should you be any less worthwhile now?

If you need additional reasons to feel good about yourself or your situation, remember that many people can't do anything as well as you can. Some people don't have their health; others do not even have their freedom. They are terrorized or locked up in cages for a good portion of their lives. Shouldn't you be thankful for your relatively good health, your lifestyle, your mental and physical skills, your opportunities, your strengths, your freedom, your friends or family, and your capacity to direct the rest of your life?

If you have gained from an experience, if it has contributed to your personal growth, if it has given you a sense of meaning (even temporarily), then it has been of some value. Draw upon the positive lessons from this experience, and get on with embracing the rest of your life and developing other competencies. Open your own doors. Recognize that as one phase of your life is ending, another phase is just beginning. Consider directing some of your hard-earned knowledge to the benefit of others—for example, by helping or teaching others, coaching a team, playing with a group of kids, giving clinics, or writing about your experiences. Your knowledge, contribution, and understanding of yourself and others can continue to grow throughout your life, long after your physical performance skills begin to decline. It is never too late to try something totally new for the sheer joy of the experience. What a beautiful feeling that can be after so many years of constant evaluation.

Some people are so afraid of looking less than perfect that they simply avoid anything in which they are not already proficient. If you have spent most of your time specializing in one activity, you may not be extremely proficient in others. Yet you can enjoy them immensely and can improve very rapidly once you make the step—once you realize that it doesn't really matter what others might expect. Who cares what others think? Their thinking can't hurt you. You don't have to be a hero. You can be whoever you want to be. Just being you, with no pretense, is fine.

Hans Selye, renowned pioneer in stress research, wrote the following words of wisdom in the introduction to his book, *The Stress of Life* (1956). "Most of our tensions and frustrations stem from compulsive needs to act the role of someone we are not. . . . 'Resolve to be thyself; and know that he who finds himself, loses his misery'" (Selye 1956). Don't let anything get in the way of your own growth and enjoyment. If you are not exceptionally proficient at something, others might even feel better and like you more. You are human just as they are—not great in everything.

For more on embracing transitions, see my book, *Embracing Your Potential: Steps to Self-Discovery, Balance, and Success in Sports, Work, and Life* (see page 235).

Chapter 22

Choosing Self-Direction

The pursuit of balanced excellence is both challenging and fulfilling. Relish its intensity, cherish its beautiful moments, and accept its risks. Many lives lack this sense of passionate absorption and personal meaning, the charged-up feeling, the flow of adrenaline, the body telling its master, *I'm ready . . . let's go.* Embrace this opportunity. Experience it and let it work for you.

Once we gain control of our inner world, competing or performing need not be the fearful experience that it has been for some people. It can be a unique opportunity to embrace the excitement, to raise your level of performance, to be stimulated by others, to test self-control, to extend limits. Meaningful challenges lead you to your personal and professional goals. They stimulate you to contribute and perform

To live your life in your own way, to reach for the goals you have set for yourself, to be the you that you want to be—that is success.

as you never have before. They bring out your best. And even if they don't, they provide lessons for living your life more fully. When you keep your sport and performance domain in perspective, you almost always emerge better from the experience.

Once you begin to view big games or important performances in a positive light, you can enjoy them more and look forward to them. The better you have prepared, the less fearful and more confident you will likely feel going into the event. But once you are there at the performance site, you have to be everything that you can do. You might as well focus on the moment and enjoy the experience, thereby freeing your body and mind to work for you. Most of us need the freedom from thoughts like "have to" or "should have" in order to deliver our best, most flowing performances.

If you find yourself questioning the value of your pursuit or your life, it is often because you are currently failing to appreciate the good things that you do have. Your focus on the negative pushes away the positive. The good is nonetheless there, though you momentarily turn your back on it. Why not open your heart to the joy of the pursuit, to the value within yourself, to the worth in others? Why not embrace your life and let the sun shine through during the challenging times as well as the joyful times? How else can you live life to the fullest?

When pursuing our life goals, we must be careful not to fall into the fatal trap that R.M. Pirsig describes in *Zen and the Art of Motorcycle Maintenance* (Pirsig 1984, 206).

> He's here but he's not here. He rejects the here, is unhappy with it, wants to be further up the trail but when he gets there will be just as unhappy because he will be "here." What he's looking for, what he wants is all around him but he doesn't want that because it is all around him. Every step's an effort, both physically and spiritually, because he imagines his goal to be external and distant.

Wherever there is only a distant destination, and no joy in the step-by-step pursuit, a harsh reality is not far behind. The real trip is in loving the journey, not necessarily in the arrival at a specific place. Unless you immerse yourself in the simple joys of your current experiences and really embrace them, dreams tend to remain dreams; worse yet, they explode or fizzle away. All the more reason to become fully absorbed in this experience, as well as many others.

As Leo Buscaglia points out in a book called *Love* (Buscaglia 1996):

> There is only the moment. The now. Only what you are experiencing at this second is real. This does not mean, live for the moment. It means live the moment. A very different thing. . . . Live now. When you are eating, eat. When you are loving, love. When you are talking to someone, talk. When you look at a flower, look. Catch the beauty of the moment.

As for change, it is inevitable. Feelings change, attitudes change, desires change, people change, love changes. We can influence the direction of change, but we cannot stop it, we cannot hold it back. Change directed toward love and self-realization is always good.

Castaneda's Don Juan speaks of it in *The Teachings of Don Juan: A Yaqui Way of Knowledge* (Castaneda 1985, 107):

> You must always keep in mind that a path is only a path. If you feel you must now follow it, you need not stay with it under any circumstances. Any path is only a path. There is no affront to yourself or others in dropping it if that is what your heart tells you to do. But your decision to keep on the path or leave it must be free of fear and ambition. I warn you: Look at every path closely and deliberately. Try it as many times as you think necessary. Then ask yourself and yourself alone one question: Does this path have a heart? All paths are the same. They lead nowhere. They are paths going through the brush or into the brush or under the brush. Does this path have a heart is the only question. If it does then the path is good . . . if it doesn't then it is of no use. Both paths lead nowhere, but one has a heart and the other doesn't. One makes for a joyful journey; as long as you follow it you will be one with it. The other will make you curse your life. One makes you strong, the other weakens you.

I used to think that the path to excellence was to work, work, work; shut out the rest of your life; and live only for the future. I was wrong! You do have to work extremely hard, but you don't have to shut out the rest of your life and you don't have to live only for the future. You can achieve the highest levels of excellence and still have a balanced and happy life in the here and now. This is the path to personal excellence, the path with a heart.

A renowned filmmaker and artist helped teach me this by example. When he worked, he became totally absorbed in his work—but he always left room for play. In fact, nothing—and I mean nothing—got

Embracing your life means living it to the fullest.

in the way of his play. His playtime enriched his life as much as any artistic achievement or outside honor bestowed upon him, probably more. It gave him something to look forward to with enthusiasm regularly, and it let him return to his work with renewed energy.

He set high goals and pursued them vigorously, but on a day-to-day basis he did not fail to appreciate his family, his own accomplishments, and the people around him. I loved going to his house to ask if the "old man" could come out to play. He appreciated each experience so much that he was a delight to be with. His enthusiasm and vitality radiated to all those around him.

He used to accuse me jokingly of sitting at home writing books about having fun and seeking balance while he was out doing it. I reflected on the way he had come to keep playfulness at the center of a life that otherwise revolved around perfection and the pursuit of excellence. A near-fatal heart attack, which almost grabbed his life, helped teach him this lesson. He was thankful for another day of living . . . then another, and another. So many days to live and experience and enjoy. A gift of life!

References and Resources

Botterill, C., and T. Patrick. 1996. *Human potential: Passion, perspective and preparation.* Winnipeg, Manitoba: Lifeskills Inc. (15 Wildwood Park, Winnipeg, Manitoba, Canada R3T 0E1).

Buscaglia, L. 1996. *Love.* Greenwich, CT: Fawcett.

Castaneda, C. 1985. *The teachings of Don Juan: A Yaqui way of knowledge.* New York: Simon & Schuster.

Colgrove, M., H. Bloomfield, and P. McWilliams. 1993. *How to survive the loss of a love.* New York: Bantam.

Ellis, A., and R.A. Harper. 1976. *A new guide to rational living.* North Hollywood, CA: Wilshire.

Frankl, V.E. 1998. *Man's search for meaning.* New York: Simon & Schuster.

Genge, R. 1976. Concentration. *Coaching Association of Canada Bulletin* 12:1-8.

Halliwell, W., T. Orlick, K. Ravizza, and B. Rotella. 1999. *Consultant's guide to excellence.* Chelsea, QC: Orlick Excel (C.P. 1807, Chelsea, QC, Canada J9B 1A1).

Orlick, E. 1999a. *How to rapidly and effectively hypnotize yourself.* Chelsea, QC: Orlick Excel.

———. 1999b. *Hypnosis: The amazing speedway to sport success.* Chelsea, QC: Orlick Excel.

Orlick, T. 1986. *Psyching for sport: Mental training for athletes.* Champaign, IL: Human Kinetics.

———. 1996. *Nice on my feelings: Nurturing the best in children and parents.* Carp, ON: Creative Bound.

———. 1998a. *Embracing your potential: Steps to self-discovery, balance, and success in sports, work, and life.* Champaign, IL: Human Kinetics.

———. 1998b. *Feeling great: Teaching children to excel at living.* Carp, ON: Creative Bound.

———. 1999. *Visions of excellence* (CD-ROM). Chelsea, QC: Orlick Excel.

Orlick, T., and J. Partington. 1986. *Psyched: Inner views of winning.* Available: **www.terryorlick.com** [September 19, 1999].

Partington, J. 1995. *Making music.* Ottawa, ON: Carleton University Press.

Pirsig, R.M. 1984. *Zen and the art of motorcycle maintenance.* New York: Quill.

Ravizza, K., and T. Hanson. 1995. *Heads-up baseball: Playing the game one pitch at a time.* Redondo Beach, CA: Kinesis (PO Box 7000-717, Redondo Beach, CA 90277).

Rotella, B., with B. Cullen. 1995. *Golf is not a game of perfect.* New York: Simon & Schuster.

Russell, B., and T. Branch. 1979. *Second wind.* New York: Ballantine.

Selye, H. 1978. *The stress of life.* New York: McGraw-Hill.

Suzuki, D.T. 1993. *Zen and Japanese culture.* New York: Pantheon.

————. 1999. Introduction to *Zen in the art of archery,* by E. Herrigel. New York: Vintage.

MENTAL TRAINING AUDIOTAPES

Available from **www.terryorlick.com** or Orlick Excel, CP 1807, Chelsea, QC, Canada J9B 1A1.

Orlick, T. 1994. *In pursuit of personal excellence—Exercises for concentration and relaxation.*

This audiotape includes 6 different scripts and activities for pursuing personal excellence: Elements of Excellence, Mental Preparation for Training, Relaxation, Pre-competition Preparation, Refocusing, and Healing. The activities take you through a series of positive exercises that will help you to achieve your personal performance goals.

————. 1996. Relaxation and stress control activities for teenagers and adults.

This audiotape is comprised of 10 different activities for relaxation and stress control: Soaring, Sea of Tranquility, Flowing Stream, Change Channels, One-Breath Relaxation, Laughing, Living Highlights, and Sea of Tranquility—The Complete Journey (three parts). The sounds, feelings, and images teach you how to relax, re-energize, and keep balance in your life.

MENTAL TRAINING ON THE INTERNET

I am now offering individualized performance enhancement consulting on the Internet for athletes and other performers. I will guide you through your personal pursuit of excellence and provide individual feedback. For more information, visit **www.terryorlick.com**, e-mail me at orlick@rems.net, or fax (819) 827-2652. or write to Orlick Excel, C.P. 1807, Chelsea, QC, Canada, J9B1A1.

Other Books by Terry Orlick

Every kid can win, with Cal Botterill, 1975.

The cooperative sports and games book, 1978.

Winning through cooperation, 1978.

The second cooperative sports and games book, 1982.

Mental training for coaches and athletes, edited with John Partington and John Salmela, 1982.

Sport in perspective, edited with John Partington and John Salmela, 1982.

New paths to sport learning, edited with John Salmela and John Partington, 1982.

Psyching for sport: Mental training for athletes, 1986.

Coaches training manual to psyching for sport, 1986.

Psyched: Inner views of winning, with John Partington, 1986.

Athletes in transition, with Penny Werthner, 1987.

Sharing views on the process of effective sportpsych consulting, with John Partington, 1988.

New beginnings: Transition from high performance sport, with Penny Werthner, 1992.

Nice on my feelings: Nurturing the best in children and parents, 1996.

In pursuit of excellence—Audio book, 1997.

Feeling great: Teaching children to excel at living, 1998.

Embracing your potential: Steps to self-discovery, balance, and success in sports, work and life, 1998.

Consultant's guide to excellence, with Wayne Halliwell, Ken Ravizza and Bob Rotella, 1999.

For further information and resources, visit my Web site: **www.terryorlick.com**

INDEX

ABOUT THE AUTHOR

Terry Orlick, PhD, is a world-renowned leader in the applied field of mental training and excellence. A former gymnastics champion and coach, Orlick has served as a sport psychology consultant for the past 28 years to hundreds of Olympic athletes in more than 25 different sports, including Alpine skiing, canoeing, figure skating, basketball, and ski jumping. He has acted as a performance enhancement consultant and mental skills coach for several Olympic Games, as well as a consultant for various professional and developmental teams.

Former president of the International Society for Mental Training and Excellence, Orlick has authored more than 20 highly acclaimed books, including *Embracing Your Potential* (1998 Human Kinetics) and *Psyching for Sport* (1986 Human Kinetics). He has created innovative programs for children and youth to develop humanistic perspectives and positive mental skills for living, and his two books, *The Cooperative Sports and Games Book* (1978 Pantheon Books) and *Feeling Great: Teaching Children to Excel at Living* (1998 Creative Bound), have had great impact on children and their quality of life.

Orlick is a professor in the School of Human Kinetics at the University of Ottawa, Canada, and founder of the innovative new *Journal of Excellence*. He holds distinguished service awards from numerous Olympic and education associations, as well as a certificate of merit from the Canadian government for distinguished service to the community. He has given lectures on the pursuit of excellence in virtually every corner of the world. Orlick lives with his family near Ottawa, Canada's capital. His leisure activities include trail running, kayaking, and experiencing daily simple joys with his family and friends. Visit his Web site at: **www.terryorlick.com**